This is a technical explanation of the Protocol signed at Berlin on June 1, 2006 (the "Protocol"), amending the Convention between the United States of America and the Federal Republic of Germany for the avoidance of double taxation and the prevention of fiscal evasion with respect to taxes on income and capital and to certain other taxes, and the related protocol, signed at Bonn on August 29, 1989 (hereinafter the "Convention" and "Protocol to the Convention" respectively).

Negotiations took into account the U.S. Department of the Treasury's current tax treaty policy and Treasury's Model Income Tax Convention, published on September 20, 1996 (the "1996 U.S. Model").1 Negotiations also took into account the Model Tax Convention on Income and on Capital, published by the Organisation for Economic Cooperation and Development (the "OECD Model"), and recent tax treaties concluded by both countries.

This Technical Explanation is an official guide to the Protocol. It explains policies behind particular provisions, as well as understandings reached during the negotiations with respect to the interpretation and application of the Protocol. This technical explanation is not intended to provide a complete guide to the Convention as amended by the Protocol. To the extent that the Convention has not been amended by the Protocol, the Technical Explanation of the Convention remains the official explanation. Moreover, Article XVI of the Protocol restates and updates the Protocol to the Convention. This technical explanation discusses only those aspects of Article XVI that amend the Protocol to the Convention. To the extent that a paragraph from the Protocol to the Convention has not been changed, the technical explanation to the Convention remains the official explanation. References in this technical explanation to "he" or "his" should be read to mean "he or she" or "his or her."

Article I

Article I of the Protocol replaces Article 1 (Personal Scope) of the Convention with a new Article 1 (General Scope).

1 Where appropriate references will also be made to Treasury's Model Income Tax Convention, published on November 15, 2006 (the "2006 U.S. Model").

Paragraph 1

Paragraph 1 of Article 1 provides that the Convention applies only to residents of the United States or the Federal Republic of Germany, except where the terms of the Convention provide otherwise. Under Article 4 (Residence), a person is generally treated as a resident of a Contracting State if that person is, under the laws of that Contracting State, liable to tax therein by reason of his domicile, residence, citizenship, place of management, place of incorporation, or other similar criteria. However, if a person is considered a resident of both Contracting States, Article 4 provides rules for determining a single Contracting State of residence (or no Contracting State of residence). This determination governs for all purposes of the Convention.

Certain provisions are applicable to persons who may not be residents of either Contracting State. For example, paragraph 1 of Article 24 (Nondiscrimination) applies to nationals of the Contracting States. Under Article 26 (Exchange of Information and Administrative Assistance), information may be exchanged with respect to residents of third states.

Paragraph 2

Paragraph 2 states the generally accepted relationship both between the Convention and domestic law of the Contracting States and between the Convention and other agreements between the Contracting States. That is, no provision in the Convention may restrict any exclusion, exemption, deduction, credit or other allowance accorded by the tax laws of the Contracting States, or (except as provided in paragraph 3 with respect to non-discrimination provisions) by any other agreement between the Contracting States.

Under paragraph 2, for example, if a deduction would be allowed under the U.S. Internal Revenue Code (the "Code") in computing the U.S. taxable income of a resident of the Federal Republic of Germany, the deduction also is allowed to that person in computing taxable income under the Convention. Paragraph 2 also means that the Convention may not increase the tax burden on a resident of a Contracting State beyond the burden determined under domestic law. Thus, a right to tax given by the Convention cannot be exercised unless that right also exists under internal law.

It follows that, under the principle of paragraph 2, a taxpayer's U.S. tax liability need not be determined under the Convention if the Code would produce a more favorable result. A taxpayer may not, however, choose among the provisions of the Code and the Convention in an inconsistent manner in order to minimize tax. For example, assume that a resident of the Federal Republic of Germany has three separate businesses in the United States. One is a profitable permanent establishment and the other two are trades or businesses that would earn taxable income under the Code but that do not meet the permanent establishment threshold tests of the Convention. One is profitable and the other incurs a loss. Under the Convention, the income of the permanent establishment is taxable in the United States, and both the profit and loss of the other two businesses are ignored. Under the Code, all three would be subject to tax, but the loss would offset the profits of the two profitable ventures. The taxpayer may not invoke the Convention to exclude the profits of the profitable trade or business and invoke the Code to claim the loss of the loss trade or business against the profit of the permanent establishment. (*See* Rev. Rul. 84-17, 1984-1 C.B. 308.) If, however, the taxpayer invokes the Code for the taxation of all three ventures, he would not be precluded from invoking the Convention with respect, for example, to any dividend income he may receive from the United States that is not effectively connected with any of his business activities in the United States.

Similarly, nothing in the Convention can be used to deny any benefit granted by any other agreement between the United States and the Federal Republic of Germany. For example, if certain benefits are provided for military personnel or military contractors under a Status of Forces Agreement between the United States and the Federal Republic of Germany, those benefits or protections will be available to residents of the Contracting States regardless of any provisions to the contrary (or silence) in the Convention.

Paragraph 3

Paragraph 3 specifically relates to non-discrimination obligations of the Contracting States under other agreements. The provisions of paragraph 3 are an exception to the rule provided in subparagraph (b) of paragraph 2 of this Article under which the Convention shall not restrict in any manner any benefit now or hereafter accorded by any other agreement between the Contracting States.

Clause (aa) of subparagraph (a) of paragraph 3 provides that, notwithstanding any other agreement to which the Contracting States may be parties, a dispute concerning the interpretation or application of the Convention, including a dispute concerning whether a taxation measure is within the scope of the Convention, shall be considered only by the competent authorities of the Contracting States, and the procedures under Article 25 (Mutual Agreement Procedure) of the Convention exclusively shall apply to the dispute. Thus, dispute-resolution procedures that may be incorporated into trade, investment, or other agreements between the Contracting States shall not apply in determining the interpretation, application, or scope of the Convention.

Clause (bb) of subparagraph (a) of paragraph 3 provides that no other agreement to which the United States and the Federal Republic of Germany are parties shall apply with respect to a taxation measure unless the competent authorities agree that the measure is not within the scope of the non-discrimination provisions of Article 24 (Nondiscrimination) of the Convention. Accordingly, if the non-discrimination provisions of this Convention apply to a taxation measure, no national treatment or most-favored-nation ("MFN") obligations undertaken by the Contracting States in any other agreement shall apply to that taxation measure.

Subparagraph (b) of paragraph 3 defines a "measure" broadly. It would include, for example, a law, regulation, rule, procedure, decision, administrative action or guidance, or any other form of measure.

Paragraph 4

Subparagraph (a) of paragraph 4 contains the traditional saving clause found in all U.S. treaties. The United States reserves the right, except as provided in paragraph 5, to tax its residents and citizens as provided in its internal law, notwithstanding any provisions of the Convention to the contrary. For example, if a resident of the Federal Republic of Germany performs professional services in the United States and the income from the services is not attributable to a permanent establishment in the United States, Article 7 (Business Profits) would by its terms prevent the United States from taxing the income. If, however, the resident of the Federal Republic of Germany is also a citizen of the United States, the saving clause permits the United States to include the remuneration in the worldwide income of the citizen and subject it to tax under the normal Code rules (*i.e.*, without regard to Code section 894(a)). However, subparagraph 5(a) of Article 1 preserves the benefits of special foreign tax credit rules applicable to the U.S. taxation of certain U.S. income of its citizens resident in the Federal Republic of Germany. *See* paragraph 5 of Article 23 (Relief from Double Taxation).

For purposes of the saving clause, "residence" is determined under Article 4 (Residence). Thus, an individual who is a resident of the United States under the Code (but not a U.S. citizen) but who is determined to be a resident of the Federal Republic of Germany under the tie-breaker rules of Article 4 would be subject to U.S. tax only to the extent permitted by the Convention. The United States would not be permitted to apply its statutory rules to that person to the extent the rules are inconsistent with the treaty.

However, the person would be treated as a U.S. resident for U.S. tax purposes other than determining the individual's U.S. tax liability. For example, in determining under Code section 957 whether a foreign corporation is a controlled foreign corporation, shares in that corporation held by the individual would be considered to be held by a U.S. resident. As a result, other U.S. citizens or residents might be deemed to be United States shareholders of a controlled foreign corporation subject to current inclusion of subpart F income recognized by the corporation. *See*, Treas. Reg. section 301.7701(b)-7(a)(3).

Subparagraph (b) provides that the United States also reserves its right to tax former citizens and former long-term residents for a period of ten years following the loss of such status. Thus, paragraph 4 allows the United States to tax former U.S. citizens and former U.S. long-term residents in accordance with section 877 of the Code. Section 877 generally applies to a former citizen or long-term resident of the United States who relinquishes citizenship or terminates long-term residency if either of the following criteria exceed established thresholds: (i) the average annual net income tax of such individual for the period of five taxable years ending before the date of the loss of status, or (ii) the net worth of such individual as of the date of the loss of status. The average annual net income tax threshold is adjusted annually for inflation.

Paragraph 1 of Article XVI of the Protocol makes clear that the definition of a "long-term resident" found in section 877 applies for purposes of subparagraph b) of paragraph 4 of Article 1. Section 877 defines a "long-term resident" as an individual (other than a U.S. citizen) who is a lawful permanent resident of the United States in at least eight of the prior 15 taxable years. An individual is not treated as a lawful permanent resident for any taxable year if such individual is treated as a resident of a foreign country under the provisions of a tax treaty between the United States and the foreign country and the individual does not waive the benefits of such treaty applicable to residents of the foreign country.

Paragraph 5

Paragraph 5 sets forth certain exceptions to the saving clause. The referenced provisions are intended to provide benefits to citizens and residents even if such benefits do not exist under internal law. Paragraph 5 thus preserves these benefits for citizens and residents of the United States.

Subparagraph (a) lists certain provisions of the Convention that are applicable to all citizens and residents of the United States, despite the general saving clause rule of paragraph 4:

(1) Paragraph 2 of Article 9 (Associated Enterprises) grants the right to a correlative adjustment with respect to income tax due on profits reallocated under Article 9.

(2) Paragraph 6 of Article 13 (Gains) provides special basis adjustment rules for the taxation of gains in a Contracting State derived by an individual who upon ceasing to be a resident of the other Contracting States is treated under the taxation laws of that State as having alienated property and is taxed in that State by reason thereof.

(3) Paragraph 3, 4 and 5 Article 18 (Pensions, Annuities, Alimony, Child Support, and Social Security) provides exemptions from source or residence State taxation for certain alimony, child support, and social security payments.

(4) Paragraph 1 of Article 18A (Pension Plans) provides an exemption for certain investment income of pension funds located in the other Contracting State, while paragraph 5 provides benefits for certain contributions by or on behalf of a U.S. citizen to certain pension funds established in the Federal Republic of Germany.

(5) Paragraph 3 of Article 19 (Government Services) provides that only the Contracting State that makes payments to a resident of the other Contracting State may tax payments which are compensation for injury or damage suffered as a result of hostility or persecution. This refers to German war reparations payments. This prevents the United States from taxing these payments even if they would be taxable under the Code.

(6) Article 23 (Relief from Double Taxation) confirms to citizens and residents of one Contracting State the benefit of a credit for income taxes paid to the other or an exemption for income earned in the other State.

(7) Article 24 (Nondiscrimination) protects residents and nationals of one Contracting State against the adoption of certain discriminatory practices in the other Contracting State.

(8) Article 25 (Mutual Agreement Procedure) confers certain benefits on citizens and residents of the Contracting States in order to reach and implement solutions to disputes between the two Contracting States. For example, the competent authorities are permitted to use a definition of a term that differs from an internal law definition. The statute of limitations may be waived for refunds, so that the benefits of an agreement may be implemented.

Subparagraph (b) of paragraph 5 provides a different set of exceptions to the saving clause. The benefits referred to are all intended to be granted to temporary residents of the United States (for example, holders of non-immigrant visas), but not to citizens or to persons who have acquired permanent resident status in the United States. If beneficiaries of these provisions travel from the Federal Republic of Germany to the United States, and remain in the United States long enough to become residents under its internal law, but do not acquire permanent residence status in the United States (i.e., they do not become "green card" holders) and are not citizens of the United States, the United State will continue to grant these benefits even if they conflict with the Code. The benefits preserved by this paragraph are: the beneficial tax treatment of pension fund contributions under paragraph 2 of Article 18A (Pension Plans), the host country exemptions for government service salaries and pensions under Article 19 (Government Service), certain income of visiting students and trainees under Article 20 (Visiting Professors and Teachers; Students and Trainees), and the income of the members of diplomatic missions and consular posts under Article 30 (Members of Diplomatic Missions and Consular Posts).

Paragraph 6

Paragraph 6 contains a rule relating to German tax. In much the same way that the saving clause preserves U.S. taxing rights with respect to its citizens and residents, this paragraph preserves German statutory rights with respect to the income of German residents. It further provides that if any tax imposed by virtue of this paragraph results in double taxation, the competent authorities will seek to eliminate the double taxation by use of the mutual agreement procedure, particularly paragraph 3 of Article 25 (Mutual Agreement Procedure) which provides, among other things, for consultation between the competent authorities to eliminate double taxation in cases not provided for in the Convention.

Paragraph 7

Paragraph 7 addresses special issues presented by fiscally transparent entities such as partnerships and certain estates and trusts. Because different countries frequently take different views as to when an entity is fiscally transparent, the risk of both double taxation and double non-taxation are relatively high. The intention of paragraph 7 is to eliminate a number of technical problems that arguably would have prevented investors using such entities from claiming treaty benefits, even though such investors would be subject to tax on the income derived through such entities. The provision also prevents the use of such entities to claim treaty benefits in circumstances where the person investing through such an entity is not subject to tax on the income in its State of residence. The provision, and the corresponding requirements of the substantive rules of Articles 6 through 21, should be read with those two goals in mind.

In general, paragraph 7 relates to entities that are not subject to tax at the entity level, as distinct from entities that are subject to tax, but with respect to which tax may be relieved under an integrated system. This paragraph applies to any resident of a Contracting State who is entitled to income derived through an entity that is treated as fiscally transparent under the laws of either Contracting State. Entities falling under this description in the United States include partnerships, common investment trusts under section 584 and grantor trusts. This paragraph also applies to U.S. limited liability companies ("LLCs") that are treated as partnerships or as disregarded entities for U.S. tax purposes.

Under paragraph 7, an item of income, profit or gain derived by such a fiscally transparent entity will be considered to be derived by a resident of a Contracting State if a resident is treated under the taxation laws of that State as deriving the item of income. For example, if a German company pays interest to an entity that is treated as fiscally transparent for U.S. tax purposes, the interest will be considered derived by a resident of the U.S. only to the extent that the taxation laws of the United States treats one or more U.S. residents (whose status as U.S. residents is determined, for this purpose, under U.S. tax law) as deriving the interest for U.S. tax purposes. In the case of a partnership, the persons who are, under U.S. tax laws, treated as partners of the entity would normally be the persons whom the U.S. tax laws would treat as deriving the interest income through the partnership. Also, it follows that persons whom the United States treats as partners but who are not U.S. residents for U.S. tax purposes may not claim a benefit for the interest paid to the entity under the Convention, because they are not residents of the United States for purposes of claiming this treaty benefit. (If, however, the country in which they are treated as resident for tax purposes, as determined under the laws of that country, has an income tax convention with the Federal Republic of Germany, they may be entitled to claim a benefit under that convention.) In contrast, if, for example, an entity is organized under U.S. laws and is classified as a corporation for U.S. tax purposes, interest paid by a German company to the U.S. entity will be considered derived by a resident of the United States since the U.S. corporation is treated under U.S. taxation laws as a resident of the United States and as deriving the income.

The same result obtains even if the entity were viewed differently under the tax laws of the country of source (*e.g.*, as not fiscally transparent in the Federal Republic of Germany in the first example above where the entity is treated as a partnership for U.S. tax purposes). Similarly, the characterization of the entity in a third country is also irrelevant, even if the entity is organized in that third country. The results follow regardless of whether the entity is disregarded as a separate entity under the laws of one jurisdiction but not the other, such as a single owner entity that is viewed as a branch for U.S. tax purposes and as a corporation for German tax purposes. These results also obtain regardless of where the entity is organized (*i.e.*, in the United States, in the Federal Republic of Germany, or, as noted above, in a third country).

For example, income from U.S. sources received by an entity organized under the laws of the United States, which is treated for German tax purposes as a corporation and is owned by a German shareholder who is a German resident for German tax purposes, is not considered derived by the shareholder of that corporation even if, under the tax laws of the United States, the entity is treated as fiscally transparent. Rather, for purposes of the treaty, the income is treated as derived by the U.S. entity.

These principles also apply to trusts to the extent that they are fiscally transparent in either Contracting State. For example, if X, a resident of the Federal Republic of Germany, creates a revocable trust in the United States and names persons resident in a third country as the beneficiaries of the trust, the trust's income would be regarded as being derived by a resident of the Federal Republic of Germany only to the extent that the laws of the Federal Republic of Germany treat X as deriving the income for its tax purposes, perhaps through application of rules similar to the U.S. "grantor trust" rules.

Paragraph 7 is not an exception to the saving clause of paragraph 4. Accordingly, paragraph 7 does not prevent the United States from taxing an entity that is treated as a resident of the United States under its tax law. For example, if a U.S. LLC with members who are residents of the Federal Republic of Germany elects to be taxed as a corporation for U.S. tax purposes, the United States will tax that LLC on its worldwide income on a net basis, without regard to whether the Federal Republic of Germany views the LLC as fiscally transparent.

Article II

Article II of the Protocol modifies Article 4 (Residence) of the Convention by replacing paragraph 1, which defines the term "resident of a Contracting State". As a general matter only residents of the Contracting States may claim the benefits of the Convention. The treaty definition of residence is to be used only for purposes of the Convention. The fact that a person is determined to be a resident of a Contracting State under Article 4 does not necessarily entitle that person to the benefits of the Convention. In addition to being a resident, a person also must qualify for benefits under Article 28 (Limitation on Benefits) in order to receive benefits conferred on residents of a Contracting State.

Paragraph 1

The term "resident of a Contracting State" is defined in paragraph 1. In general, this definition incorporates the definitions of residence in U.S. and German law by referring to a resident as a person who, under the laws of a Contracting State, is subject to tax therein by reason of his domicile, residence, place of management, place of incorporation or any other similar criterion. Thus, residents of the United States generally include U.S. citizens, U.S. green card holders, and aliens who are considered U.S. residents under Code section 7701(b). Paragraph 1 also specifically includes the United States, the Federal Republic of Germany, and political subdivisions and local authorities of the two States as residents for purposes of the Convention.

Certain entities that are nominally subject to tax but that in practice are rarely required to pay tax also would generally be treated as residents and therefore accorded treaty benefits. For example, a U.S. Regulated Investment Company (RIC) and a U.S. Real Estate Investment Trust (REIT) are residents of the United States for purposes of the treaty. Although the income earned by these entities normally is not subject to U.S. tax in the hands of the entity, they are taxable to the extent that they do not currently distribute their profits, and therefore may be regarded as "liable to tax." They also must satisfy a number of requirements under the Code in order to be entitled to special tax treatment. Subparagraph b) of paragraph 2 of Article XVI of the Protocol clarifies that, for purposes of the Convention, German Investment Funds and German *Investmentaktiengesellschaft* (collectively referred to as *Investmentvermögen*) created under the provisions of the Investment Act of 2003 (*Investmentgesetz*) are residents of the Federal Republic of Germany and that a U.S. RIC and a U.S. REIT are also residents of the United States.

A person who is liable to tax in a Contracting State only in respect of income from sources within that State or capital situated therein or of profits attributable to a permanent establishment in that State will not be treated as a resident of that Contracting State for purposes of the Convention. Thus, a consular official of the Federal Republic of Germany who is posted in the United States, who may be subject to U.S. tax on U.S. source investment income, but is not taxable in the United States on non-U.S. source income (see Code section 7701(b)(5)(B)), would not be considered a resident of the United States for purposes of the Convention. Similarly, an enterprise of the Federal Republic of Germany with a permanent establishment in the United States is not, by virtue of that permanent establishment, a resident of the United States. The enterprise generally is subject to U.S. tax only with respect to its income that is attributable to the U.S. permanent establishment, not with respect to its worldwide income, as it would be if it were a U.S. resident.

Subparagraph a) of paragraph 2 of Article XVI of the Protocol provides the Federal Republic of Germany shall treat a United States citizen or alien lawfully admitted for permanent residence (a "green card holder") as a resident of the United States only if such person has a substantial presence (see section 7701(b)(3)), permanent home, or habitual abode in the United States. This rule requires that the U.S. citizen or green card holder have a reasonably strong economic nexus with the United States in order to claim German treaty benefits under the Convention.

Article III

Paragraph a) of Article III of the Protocol replaces paragraph 3 of Article 7 (Business Profits) of the Convention. This paragraph is the same as paragraph 3 of Article 7 of the 2006 U.S. Model. Paragraph 3 provides that in determining the business profits of a permanent establishment, deductions shall be allowed for the expenses incurred for the purposes of the permanent establishment, ensuring that business profits will be taxed on a net basis. This rule is not limited to expenses incurred exclusively for the purposes of the permanent establishment, but includes expenses incurred for the purposes of the enterprise as a whole, or that part of the enterprise that includes the permanent establishment. Deductions are to be allowed regardless of which accounting unit of the enterprise books the expenses, so long as they are incurred for the purposes of the permanent establishment. For example, a portion of the interest expense recorded on the books of the home office in one State may be deducted by a permanent establishment in the other if properly allocable thereto. The amount of expense that must be allowed as a deduction is determined by applying the arm's length principle.

Paragraph 4 of Article XVI of the Protocol provides rules for the attribution of business profits to a permanent establishment. The Contracting States will attribute to a permanent establishment the profits that it would have earned had it been a distinct and separate enterprise engaged in the same or similar activities under the same or similar conditions and dealing wholly independently with the enterprise of which it is a permanent establishment.

Paragraph 4 of Article XVI of the Protocol states that it is understood that the business profits to be attributed to a permanent establishment shall include only the profits derived from the assets used, risks assumed, and activities performed by the permanent establishment. In addition, the OECD Transfer Pricing Guidelines apply, by analogy, in determining the profits attributable to a permanent establishment. Accordingly, a permanent establishment may deduct payments made to its head office or another branch in compensation for services performed for the benefit of the branch. The method to be used in calculating that amount will depend on the terms of the arrangements between the branches and head office. For example, the enterprise could have a policy, expressed in writing, under which each business unit could use the services of lawyers employed by the head office. At the end of each year, the costs of employing the lawyers would be allocated to each business unit according to the amount of services used by that business unit during the year. Since this appears to be a kind of cost-sharing arrangement and the allocation of costs is based on the benefits received by each business unit, it would be an acceptable means of determining a permanent establishment's deduction for legal expenses. Alternatively, the head office could agree to employ lawyers at its own risk, and to charge an arm's length price for legal services performed for a particular business unit. If the lawyers were under-utilized, and the "fees" received from the business units were less than the cost of employing the lawyers, then the head office would bear the excess cost. If the "fees" exceeded the cost of employing the lawyers, then the head office would keep the excess to compensate it for assuming the risk of employing the lawyers. If the enterprise acted in accordance with this agreement, this method would be an acceptable alternative method for calculating a permanent establishment's deduction for legal expenses.

The permanent establishment cannot be funded entirely with debt, but must have sufficient capital to carry on its activities as if it were a distinct and separate enterprise. To the extent that the permanent establishment does not have such capital, a Contracting State may attribute such capital to the permanent establishment and deny an interest deduction to the extent necessary to reflect that capital attribution. The method prescribed by U.S. domestic law for making this attribution is found in Treas. Reg. § 1.882-5. Both § 1.882-5 and the method prescribed in the Protocol start from the premise that all of the capital of the enterprise supports all of the assets and risks of the enterprise, and therefore the entire capital of the enterprise must be allocated to its various businesses and offices.

However, § 1.882-5 does not take into account the fact that some assets create more risk for the enterprise than do other assets. An independent enterprise would need less capital to support a perfectly-hedged U.S. Treasury security than it would need to support an equity security or other asset with significant market and/or credit risk. Accordingly, in some cases § 1.882-5 would require a taxpayer to allocate more capital to the United States, and therefore would reduce the taxpayer's interest deduction more, than is appropriate. To address these cases, paragraph 4 of Article XVI of the Protocol allows a taxpayer to apply a more flexible approach that takes into account the relative risk of its assets in the various jurisdictions in which it does business. In particular, in the case of financial institutions other than insurance companies, the amount of capital attributable to a permanent establishment is determined by allocating the institution's total equity between its various offices on the basis of the proportion of the financial institution's risk-weighted assets attributable to each of them. This recognizes the fact that financial institutions are in many cases required to risk-weight their assets for regulatory purposes and, in other cases, will do so for business reasons even if not required to do so by regulators. However, risk-weighting is more complicated than the method prescribed by § 1.882-5. Accordingly, to ease this administrative burden, taxpayers may choose to apply the principles of Treas. Reg. § 1.882-5(c) to determine the amount of capital allocable to its U.S. permanent establishment, in lieu of determining its allocable capital under the risk-weighed capital allocation method provided by the Protocol, even if it has otherwise chosen to apply the principles of Article 7 rather than the effectively connected income rules of U.S. domestic law.

Paragraph 4 of Article XVI of the Protocol provides an alternative to the analogous but somewhat different "effectively connected" concept in Code section 864(c). In effect, the Protocol allows the United States to tax the lesser of two amounts of income: the amount determined by applying U.S. rules regarding the calculation of effectively connected income and the amount determined under the Protocol. That is, a

11

taxpayer may choose the set of rules that results in the lowest amount of taxable income, but may not mix and match.

In some cases, the amount of income "attributable to" a permanent establishment under the Protocol may be greater than the amount of income that would be treated as "effectively connected" to a U.S. trade or business under section 864. For example, a taxpayer that has a significant amount of foreign source royalty income attributable to a U.S. branch may find that it will pay less tax in the United States by applying section 864(c) of the Code, rather than the rules of the Protocol, if the foreign source royalties are not derived in the active conduct of a trade or business and thus would not be effectively connected income. But, as described in the Technical Explanation to Article 1(2), if it does so, it may not then use the Protocol principles to exempt other income that would be effectively connected to the U.S. trade or business. Conversely, if it uses the Protocol principles to exempt other effectively connected income that is not attributable to its U.S. permanent establishment, then it must include the foreign source royalties in its net taxable income even though such royalties would not constitute effectively connected income.

In the case of financial institutions, the use of internal dealings to allocate income within an enterprise may produce results under the Protocol that are significantly different than the results under the effectively connected income rules. For example, income from interbranch notional principal contracts may be taken into account under the Protocol, notwithstanding that such transactions may be ignored for purposes of U.S. domestic law. Under the consistency rule described above, a financial institution that conducts different lines of business through its U.S. permanent establishment may not choose to apply the rules of the Code with respect to some lines of business and the Protocol of the Convention with respect to others. If it chooses to use the rules of the Protocol to allocate its income from its trading book, it may not then use U.S. domestic rules to allocate income from its loan portfolio.

The profits attributable to a permanent establishment may be from sources within or without a Contracting State. However, as stated in the Protocol, the business profits attributable to a permanent establishment include only those profits derived from the assets used, risks assumed, and activities performed by, the permanent establishment.

The language of the Protocol, when combined with paragraph 3 dealing with the allowance of deductions for expenses incurred for the purposes of earning the profits, incorporates the arm's-length standard for purposes of determining the profits attributable to a permanent establishment. As noted below with respect to Article 9, the United States generally interprets the arm's length standard in a manner consistent with the OECD Transfer Pricing Guidelines.

The arm's length method consists of applying the OECD Transfer Pricing Guidelines, but taking into account the different economic and legal circumstances of a single legal entity (as opposed to separate but associated enterprises). Thus, any of the methods used in the Transfer Pricing Guidelines, including profits methods, may be used as appropriate and in accordance with the Transfer Pricing Guidelines. However, the use of the Transfer Pricing Guidelines applies only for purposes of attributing profits within the legal entity. It does not create legal obligations or other tax consequences that would result from transactions having independent legal significance.

For example, an entity that operates through branches rather than separate subsidiaries will have lower capital requirements because all of the assets of the entity are available to support all of the entity's liabilities (with some exceptions attributable to local regulatory restrictions). This is the reason that most commercial banks and some insurance companies operate through branches rather than subsidiaries. The benefit that comes from such lower capital costs must be allocated among the branches in an appropriate manner. This issue does not arise in the case of an enterprise that operates through separate entities, since each entity will have to be separately capitalized or will have to compensate another entity for providing capital (usually through a guarantee).

Under U.S. domestic regulations, internal "transactions" generally are not recognized because they do not have legal significance. In contrast, the rule provided by the Protocol is that such internal dealings may be used to allocate income in cases where the dealings accurately reflect the allocation of risk within the enterprise. One example is that of global trading in securities. In many cases, banks use internal swap transactions to transfer risk from one branch to a central location where traders have the expertise to manage that particular type of risk. Under the Convention, such a bank may also use such swap transactions as a means of allocating income between the branches, if use of that method is the "best method" within the meaning of regulation section 1.482-1(c). The books of a branch will not be respected, however, when the results are inconsistent with a functional analysis. So, for example, income from a transaction that is booked in a particular branch (or home office) will not be treated as attributable to that location if the sales and risk management functions that generate the income are performed in another location.

Because the use of profits methods is permissible under the Protocol, it is not necessary for the Convention to include a provision corresponding to paragraph 4 of Article 7 of the OECD Model.

Paragraph b) of Article III of the Protocol provides that income from the performance of professional services and other activities of an independent character are business profits.

Article IV

Article IV of the Protocol replaces Article 10 (Dividends) of the Convention. Article 10 provides rules for the taxation of dividends paid by a company that is a resident of one Contracting State to a beneficial owner that is a resident of the other Contracting State. The article provides for full residence country taxation of such dividends and a limited source-State right to tax. Article 10 also provides rules for the imposition of a tax on branch profits by the State of source. Finally, the article prohibits a State from imposing taxes on a company resident in the other Contracting State, other than a branch profits tax, on undistributed earnings.

Paragraph 1

The right of a shareholder's country of residence to tax dividends arising in the source country is preserved by paragraph 1, which permits a Contracting State to tax its residents on dividends paid to them by a company that is a resident of the other Contracting State. For dividends from any other source paid to a resident, Article 21 (Other Income) grants the residence country exclusive taxing jurisdiction (other than for dividends attributable to a permanent establishment in the other State).

Paragraph 2

The State of source also may tax dividends beneficially owned by a resident of the other State, subject to the limitations of paragraphs 2 and 3. Paragraph 2 generally limits the rate of withholding tax in the State of source on dividends paid by a company resident in that State to 15 percent of the gross amount of the dividend. If, however, the beneficial owner of the dividend is a company resident in the other State and owns directly shares representing at least 10 percent of the voting power of the company paying the dividend, then the rate of withholding tax in the State of source is limited to 5 percent of the gross amount of the dividend. Shares are considered voting shares if they provide the power to elect, appoint or replace any person vested with the powers ordinarily exercised by the board of directors of a U.S. corporation.

The benefits of paragraph 2 may be granted at the time of payment by means of reduced rate of withholding tax at source. It also is consistent with the paragraph for tax to be withheld at the time of payment at full statutory rates, and the treaty benefit to be granted by means of a subsequent refund so long as such procedures are applied in a reasonable manner.

The determination of whether the ownership threshold for subparagraph (a) of paragraph 2 is met for purposes of the 5 percent maximum rate of withholding tax is made on the date on which entitlement to the dividend is determined. Thus, in the case of a dividend from a U.S. company, the determination of whether the ownership threshold is met generally would be made on the dividend record date.

Paragraph 2 does not affect the taxation of the profits out of which the dividends are paid. The taxation by a Contracting State of the income of its resident companies is governed by the internal law of the Contracting State, subject to the provisions of paragraph 4 of Article 24 (Nondiscrimination).

The term "beneficial owner" is not defined in the Convention, and is, therefore, defined as under the internal law of the country imposing tax (*i.e.*, the source country). The beneficial owner of the dividend for purposes of Article 10 is the person to which the dividend income is attributable under the laws of the source State. Thus, if a dividend

14

paid by a corporation that is a resident of one of the States (as determined under Article 4 (Residence)) is received by a nominee or agent that is a resident of the other State on behalf of a person that is not a resident of that other State, the dividend is not entitled to the benefits of this Article. However, a dividend received by a nominee on behalf of a resident of that other State would be entitled to benefits. These limitations are confirmed by paragraph 12 of the Commentary to Article 10 of the OECD Model.

Companies holding shares through fiscally transparent entities such as partnerships are considered for purposes of this paragraph to hold their proportionate interest in the shares held by the intermediate entity. As a result, companies holding shares through such entities may be able to claim the benefits of subparagraph (a) under certain circumstances. The lower rate applies when the company's proportionate share of the shares held by the intermediate entity meets the 10 percent threshold, and the company meets the requirements of Article 1(7) (i.e., the company's country of residence treats the intermediate entity as fiscally transparent) with respect to the dividend. Whether this ownership threshold is satisfied may be difficult to determine and often will require an analysis of the partnership or trust agreement.

Paragraph 3

Paragraph 3 provides exclusive residence-country taxation (*i.e.,* an elimination of withholding tax) with respect to certain dividends distributed by a company that is a resident of one Contracting State to a resident of the other Contracting State. As described further below, this elimination of withholding tax is available with respect to certain inter-company dividends and with respect to certain pension funds.

Subparagraph (a) of paragraph 3 provides for the elimination of withholding tax on dividends beneficially owned by a company that has owned 80 percent or more of the voting power of the company paying the dividend for the 12-month period ending on the date entitlement to the dividend is determined. The determination of whether the beneficial owner of the dividends owns at least 80 percent of the voting power of the paying company is made by taking into account only stock owned directly.

Eligibility for the elimination of withholding tax provided by subparagraph (a) is subject to additional restrictions based on, but supplementing, the rules of Article 28 (Limitation on Benefits). Accordingly, a company that meets the holding requirements described above will qualify for the benefits of paragraph 3 only if it also: (1) meets the "publicly traded" test of subparagraph 2(c) of Article 28 (Limitation on Benefits), (2) meets the "ownership-base erosion" and "active trade or business" tests described in subparagraph 2(f) and paragraph 4 of Article 28 (Limitation on Benefits), (3) meets the "derivative benefits" test of paragraph 3 of Article 28 (Limitation on Benefits), or (4) is granted the benefits of subparagraph 3(a) of Article 10 by the competent authority of the source State pursuant to paragraph 7 of Article 28 (Limitation on Benefits).

These restrictions are necessary because of the increased pressure on the Limitation on Benefits tests resulting from the fact that the United States has relatively few treaties that provide for such elimination of withholding tax on inter-company dividends. The additional restrictions are intended to prevent companies from re-organizing in order to become eligible for the elimination of withholding tax in circumstances where the Limitation on Benefits provision does not provide sufficient protection against treaty-shopping.

For example, assume that ThirdCo is a company resident in a third country that does not have a tax treaty with the United States providing for the elimination of withholding tax on inter-company dividends. ThirdCo owns directly 100 percent of the issued and outstanding voting stock of USCo, a U.S. company, and of GCo, a German company. GCo is a substantial company that manufactures widgets; USCo distributes those widgets in the United States. If ThirdCo contributes to GCo all the stock of USCo, dividends paid by USCo to GCo would qualify for treaty benefits under the active trade or business test of paragraph 4 of Article 28. However, allowing ThirdCo to qualify for the elimination of withholding tax, which is not available to it under the third state's treaty with the United States (if any), would encourage treaty-shopping.

In order to prevent this type of treaty-shopping, paragraph 3 requires GCo to meet the ownership-base erosion requirements of subparagraph 2(f) of Article 28 in addition to the active trade or business test of paragraph 4 of Article 28. Because GCo is wholly owned by a third country resident, GCo could not qualify for the elimination of withholding tax on dividends from USCo under the combined ownership-base erosion and active trade or business tests of paragraph 3(a)(bb). Consequently, GCo would need to qualify under another test in paragraph 3(a) or obtain discretionary relief from the competent authority under Article 28(7). For purpose of Article 3(a)(bb), it is not sufficient for a company to qualify for treaty benefits generally under the active trade or business test or the ownership-base erosion test unless it qualifies for treaty benefits under both.

Alternatively, companies that are publicly traded or subsidiaries of publicly-traded companies will generally qualify for the elimination of withholding tax. Thus, a company that is a resident of the Federal Republic of Germany and that meets the requirements of Article 28(2)(c)(aa) or (bb) will be entitled to the elimination of withholding tax, subject to the 12-month holding period requirement of Article 10(3)(a).

In addition, under Article 10(3)(a)(cc), a company that is a resident of a Contracting State may also qualify for the elimination of withholding tax on dividends if it satisfies the derivative benefits test of paragraph 3 of Article 28. Thus, a German company that owns all of the stock of a U.S. corporation may qualify for the elimination of withholding tax if it is wholly-owned, for example, by a U.K., Dutch, Mexican or a Swedish publicly-traded company and the other requirements of the derivative benefits test are met. At this time, ownership by companies that are residents of other European Union, European Economic Area or North American Free Trade Agreement countries would not qualify the German company for benefits under this provision, as the United States does not have treaties that eliminate the withholding tax on inter-company dividends with any other of those countries. If the United States were to enter into such treaties with more of those countries, residents of those countries could then qualify as equivalent beneficiaries for purposes of this provision.

The derivative benefits test may also provide benefits to U.S. companies receiving dividends from German subsidiaries, because of the effect of the Parent-Subsidiary Directive in the European Union. Under that directive, inter-company dividends paid within the European Union are free of withholding tax. Under subparagraph (f) of paragraph 8 of Article 28 that directive will also be taken into account in determining whether the owner of a U.S. company receiving dividends from a German company is an "equivalent beneficiary." Thus, a company that is a resident of a member state of the European Union will, by definition, meet the requirements regarding equivalent benefits with respect to any dividends received by its U.S. subsidiary from a German company. For example, assume USCo is a wholly-owned subsidiary of ICo, an Italian publicly-traded company. USCo owns all of the shares of GCo, a German company. If GCo were to pay dividends directly to ICo, those dividends would be exempt from withholding tax in the Federal Republic of Germany by reason of the Parent-Subsidiary Directive. If ICo meets the other conditions to be an equivalent beneficiary under subparagraph 8(e) of Article 28, it will be treated as an equivalent beneficiary by reason of subparagraph 8(f) of that article.

A company also may qualify for the elimination of withholding tax pursuant to Article 10(3)(a)(cc) if it is owned by seven or fewer U.S. or German residents who qualify as an "equivalent beneficiary" and meet the other requirements of the derivative benefits provision. This rule may apply, for example, to certain German corporate joint venture vehicles that are closely-held by a few German resident individuals.

Article 28(e) contains a specific rule of application intended to ensure that for purposes of applying Article 10(3) certain joint ventures, not just wholly-owned subsidiaries, can qualify for benefits. For example, assume that the United States were to enter into a treaty with Country X, a member of the European Union, that includes a provision identical to Article 10(3). USCo is 100 percent owned by GCo, a German company, which in turn is owned 49 percent by PCo, a German publicly-traded company, and 51 percent by XCo, a publicly-traded company that is resident in Country X. In the absence of a special rule for interpreting the derivative benefits provision, each of PCo and XCo would be treated as owning only their proportionate share of the shares held by GCo in USCo. If that rule were applied in this situation, neither PCo nor XCo would be an equivalent beneficiary, because neither would meet the 80 percent ownership test with respect to USCo. However, since both PCo and XCo are residents of countries that have treaties with the United States that provide for elimination of withholding tax on inter-company dividends, it is appropriate to provide benefits to GCo in this case.

Accordingly, the definition of "equivalent beneficiary" includes a rule of application that is intended to ensure that such joint ventures qualify for the benefits of Article 10(3). Under that rule, each of the shareholders is treated as owning shares of USCo with the same percentage of voting power as the shares held by GCo for purposes of determining whether it would be entitled to an equivalent rate of withholding tax. This rule is necessary because of the high ownership threshold for qualification for the elimination of withholding tax on inter-company dividends.

If a company does not qualify for the elimination of withholding tax under any of the foregoing objective tests, it may request a determination from the relevant competent authority pursuant to paragraph 7 of Article 28. Benefits will be granted with respect to an item of income if the competent authority of the Contracting State in which the income arises determines that the establishment, acquisition or maintenance of such resident and the conduct of its operations did not have as one of its principal purposes the obtaining of benefits under the Convention.

Subparagraph (b) of paragraph 3 of Article 10 provides that dividends received by a pension fund may not be taxed in the Contracting State of which the company paying the dividend is a resident, unless such dividends are derived from the carrying on of a business, directly or indirectly, by the pension fund.

The rule is necessary because pension funds normally do not pay tax (either through a general exemption or because reserves for future pension liabilities effectively offset all of the fund's income), and therefore cannot benefit from a foreign tax credit. Moreover, distributions from a pension fund generally do not maintain the character of the underlying income, so the beneficiaries of the pension are not in a position to claim a foreign tax credit when they finally receive the pension, in many cases years after the withholding tax has been paid. Accordingly, in the absence of this rule, the dividends would almost certainly be subject to unrelieved double taxation.

Clause b) of paragraph 8 of Article XVI of the Protocol provides that in the case of Germany, subparagraph (b) of paragraph 3 of Article 10 applies to the person treated as owning the assets of the pension fund under section 39 of the Fiscal Code, provided that the dividends may only be used for providing retirement benefits through such fund. This provision makes clear that in the case of Germany, the zero rate of withholding tax for dividends paid to pension funds is also available in the case of an employer that has not set up a pension fund, but commits to pay a certain level of retirement income to its employees as described in sec. 6a of the Income Tax Act and for which the employer has established a contractual trust arrangement so long as sec. 39 of the Fiscal Code provides that for tax purposes the assets are attributable to the employer that entered into the contractual trust arrangement. For these purposes, the term "pension fund" is defined in paragraph 11 of Article 10.

Paragraph 4

Article 10 generally applies to distributions made by a RIC or a REIT. However, distributions made by a REIT or certain RICs that are attributable to gains derived from the alienation of U.S. real property interests and treated as gain recognized under section 897(h)(1) are taxable under paragraph 1 of Article 13 instead of Article 10. In the case of RIC or REIT distributions to which Article 10 applies, paragraph 4 imposes limitations on the rate reductions provided by paragraphs 2 and 3 in the case of dividends paid by a RIC or a REIT.

The first sentence of subparagraph 4 provides that dividends paid by a RIC or REIT or a German Investment Fund or a German *Investmentaktiengesellschaft* (collectively referred to as *Investmentvermögen*) are not eligible for the 5 percent rate of withholding tax of subparagraph 2(a) or the elimination of source-country withholding tax of subparagraph 3(a).

The second sentence of subparagraph 4(a) provides that the 15 percent maximum rate of withholding tax of subparagraph 2(b) applies to dividends paid by RICs and *Investmentvermögen* and that the elimination of source-country withholding tax of subparagraph 3(b) applies to dividends paid by such RICs and *Investmentvermögen* and beneficially owned by a pension fund.

The third sentence of subparagraph 4(a) provides that the 15 percent rate of withholding tax also applies to dividends paid by a REIT and that the elimination of source-country withholding tax of subparagraph 3(b) applies to dividends paid by REITs and beneficially owned by a pension fund, provided that one of the three following conditions is met. First, the beneficial owner of the dividend is an individual or a pension fund, in either case holding an interest of not more than 10 percent in the REIT. Second, the dividend is paid with respect to a class of stock that is publicly traded and the beneficial owner of the dividend is a person holding an interest of not more than 5 percent of any class of the REIT's shares. Third, the beneficial owner of the dividend holds an interest in the REIT of not more than 10 percent and the REIT is "diversified."

Paragraph 4 provides a definition of the term "diversified", which is necessary because the term is not defined in the Code. A REIT is diversified if the gross value of no single interest in real property held by the REIT exceeds 10 percent of the gross value of the REIT's total interest in real property. Foreclosure property is not considered an interest in real property, and a REIT holding a partnership interest is treated as owning its proportionate share of any interest in real property held by the partnership.

The restrictions set out above are intended to prevent the use of these entities to gain inappropriate U.S. tax benefits. For example, a company resident in the Federal Republic of Germany that wishes to hold a diversified portfolio of U.S. corporate shares could hold the portfolio directly and would bear a U.S. withholding tax of 15 percent on all of the dividends that it receives. Alternatively, it could hold the same diversified portfolio by purchasing 10 percent or more of the interests in a RIC. If the RIC is a pure conduit, there may be no U.S. tax cost to interposing the RIC in the chain of ownership. Absent the special rule in paragraph 4, such use of the RIC could transform portfolio dividends, taxable in the United States under the Convention at a 15 percent maximum rate of withholding tax, into direct investment dividends taxable at a 5 percent maximum rate of withholding tax or eligible under paragraph 3(a) for the elimination of source-country withholding tax.

Similarly, a resident of the Federal Republic of Germany directly holding U.S. real property would pay U.S. tax on rental income either at a 30 percent rate of withholding tax on the gross income or at graduated rates on the net income. As in the

19

preceding example, by placing the real property in a REIT, the investor could, absent a special rule, transform rental income into dividend income from the REIT, taxable at the rates provided in Article 10, significantly reducing the U.S. tax that otherwise would be imposed. Paragraph 4 prevents this result and thereby avoids a disparity between the taxation of direct real estate investments and real estate investments made through REIT conduits. In the cases in which paragraph 4 allows a dividend from a REIT to be eligible for the 15 percent rate of withholding tax, the holding in the REIT is not considered the equivalent of a direct holding in the underlying real property.

The same reasoning explains the treatment of U.S. REIT dividends to a pension fund. In the cases in which paragraph 4 allows a dividend from a REIT paid to a pension fund to be eligible for the zero rate of withholding tax, the holding in the REIT is also not considered the equivalent of a direct holding in the underlying real property. Although the third sentence of subparagraph 4(a) of Article 10 with respect to the elimination of source-country withholding tax of dividends paid by REITs to pension funds is by its terms bilateral, the domestic law of the Federal Republic of Germany does not currently provide for the exemption from tax of REITs. In addition, paragraph 8 of Article XVI of the Protocol provides that in the event the Federal Republic of Germany enacts such legislation, subparagraph (b) of paragraph 3 of Article 10 will not apply to dividends paid by such a company that is a resident of the Federal Republic of Germany.

Paragraph 5

Paragraph 5 defines the term dividends broadly and flexibly. The definition is intended to cover all arrangements that yield a return on an equity investment in a corporation as determined under the tax law of the state of source, as well as arrangements that might be developed in the future.

The term includes income from shares, or other corporate rights that are not treated as debt under the law of the source State, that participate in the profits of the company. The term also includes income that is subjected to the same tax treatment as income from shares by the law of the State of source. Thus, a constructive dividend that results from a non-arm's length transaction between a corporation and a related party is a dividend. In the case of the Federal Republic of Germany dividends also include income from sleeping partnerships, a participating loan, a "*Gewinnobligation*" as well as distributions on certificates of a German *Investmentvermögen*. In the case of the United States the term dividend includes amounts treated as a dividend under U.S. law upon the sale or redemption of shares or upon a transfer of shares in a reorganization. *See*, e.g., Rev. Rul. 92-85, 1992-2 C.B. 69 (sale of foreign subsidiary's stock to U.S. sister company is a deemed dividend to extent of the subsidiary's and sister company's earnings and profits). Further, a distribution from a U.S. publicly traded limited partnership, which is taxed as a corporation under U.S. law, is a dividend for purposes of Article 10. However, a distribution by a limited liability company is not taxable by the United States under Article 10, provided the limited liability company is not characterized as an association taxable as a corporation under U.S. law.

Finally, a payment denominated as interest that is made by a thinly capitalized corporation may be treated as a dividend to the extent that the debt is recharacterized as equity under the laws of the source State.

Paragraph 6

Paragraph 6 provides that the income from arrangements that carry the right to participate in profits that are deductible in the determining the profits of the payor may be taxed by the source country according to its domestic law. In the United States, these amounts include contingent interest of a type that would not qualify as portfolio interest. In the Federal Republic of Germany, these amounts include income under a sleeping partnership, a participating loan or a "*Gewinnobligation*" or "*jouissance*" shares or rights. This rule applies notwithstanding the provisions of paragraph 2 and 3 of this Article and paragraph 1 of Article 11 (Interest).

Paragraph 7

Paragraph 7 provides that the general source country limitations under paragraphs 2 through 4 on dividends do not apply if the beneficial owner of the dividends is a permanent establishment situated in the source country and the dividends are attributable to such permanent establishment. In such case, the rules of Article 7 (Business Profits) shall apply. Accordingly, such dividends will be taxed on a net basis using the rates and rules of taxation generally applicable to residents of the Contracting State in which the permanent establishment is located, as modified by the Convention. An example of dividends attributable to a permanent establishment would be dividends derived by a dealer in stock or securities from stock or securities that the dealer held for sale to customers.

Paragraph 8

The right of a Contracting State to tax dividends paid by a company that is a resident of the other Contracting State is restricted by paragraph 8 to cases in which the dividends are paid to a resident of that Contracting State or are attributable to a permanent establishment in that Contracting State. Thus, a Contracting State may not impose a "secondary" withholding tax on dividends paid by a nonresident company out of earnings and profits from that Contracting State. In the case of the United States, the secondary withholding tax was eliminated for payments made after December 31, 2004 in the American Jobs Creation Act of 2004.

The paragraph also restricts the right of a Contracting State to impose corporate level taxes on undistributed profits of a company that is a resident of the other Contracting State, other than a branch profits tax. The paragraph does not restrict a State's right to tax its resident shareholders on undistributed earnings of a corporation resident in the other State. Thus, the authority of the United States to impose taxes on subpart F income and on earnings deemed invested in U.S. property, and its tax on income of a passive foreign investment company that is a qualified electing fund is in no way restricted by this provision.

Paragraphs 9 and 10

Paragraph 9 permits a Contracting State to impose a branch profits tax on a company resident in the other Contracting State. The tax is in addition to other taxes permitted by the Convention. The term "company" is defined in subparagraph 1(e) of Article 3 (General Definitions) of the Convention.

A Contracting State may impose a branch profits tax on a company if the company has income attributable to a permanent establishment in that Contracting State, derives income from real property in that Contracting State that is taxed on a net basis under Article 6 (Income from Immovable (Real) Property), or realizes gains taxable in that State under paragraph 1 of Article 13 (Gains). In the case of the United States, the imposition of such tax is limited, however, to the portion of the aforementioned items of income that represents the amount of such income that is the "dividend equivalent amount." This is consistent with the relevant rules under the U.S. branch profits tax, and the term dividend equivalent amount is defined under U.S. law. Section 884 of the Code defines the dividend equivalent amount as an amount for a particular year that is equivalent to the income described above that is included in the corporation's effectively connected earnings and profits for that year, after payment of the corporate tax under Articles 6 (Income from Immovable (Real) Property), 7 (Business Profits) or 13 (Gains), reduced for any increase in the branch's U.S. net equity during the year or increased for any reduction in its U.S. net equity during the year. U.S. net equity is U.S. assets less U.S. liabilities. *See* Treas. Reg. section 1.884-1. Paragraph 9 of Article XVI of the Protocol clarifies that the general principle of the "dividend equivalent amount" under U.S. law is to approximate that portion of the income described in paragraph 9 of Article 10 (Dividends) that is comparable to the amount that would be distributed as a dividend if such income were earned by a locally incorporated subsidiary. Thus, the dividend equivalent amount for any year approximates the dividend that a U.S. branch office would have paid during the year if the branch had been operated as a separate U.S. subsidiary company.

The Federal Republic of Germany currently does not impose a branch profits tax. If the Federal Republic of Germany were to impose such a tax, the base is limited to the portion of the income described in subparagraph 9(a) that is comparable to the amount that would be distributed as a dividend by a locally incorporated subsidiary.

As discussed in the Technical Explanations to Articles 1(2) and Paragraph 4 of Article XVI of the Protocol, consistency principles require that a taxpayer may not mix and match the rules of the Code and the Convention in an inconsistent manner. In the context of the branch profits tax, the consistency requirement means that an enterprise that uses the principles of Article 7 to determine its net taxable income also must use those principles in determining the dividend equivalent amount. Similarly, an enterprise that uses U.S. domestic law to determine its net taxable income must also use U.S.

domestic law in complying with the branch profits tax. As in the case of Article 7, if an enterprise switches between domestic law and treaty principles from year to year, it will need to make appropriate adjustments or recapture amounts that otherwise might go untaxed.

Paragraph 10 limits the rate of the branch profits tax allowed under paragraph 9 to 5 percent. Paragraph 10 also provides that the branch profits tax shall not be imposed, however, if certain requirements are met. In general, these requirements provide rules for a branch that parallel the rules for when a dividend paid by a subsidiary will be subject to exclusive residence-country taxation (i.e., the elimination of source-country withholding tax). Accordingly, the branch profits tax may not be imposed in the case of a company that: (1) meets the "publicly traded" test of subparagraph 2(c) of Article 28 (Limitation on Benefits), (2) meets the "ownership-base erosion" and "active trade or business" tests described in subparagraph 2(f) and paragraph 4 of Article 28 (Limitation on Benefits), (3) meets the "derivative benefits" test of paragraph 3 of Article 28 (Limitation on Benefits), or (4) is granted benefits with respect to the elimination of the branch profits tax by the competent authority pursuant to paragraph 7 of Article 28 (Limitation on Benefits).

Thus, for example, if a German company would be subject to the branch profits tax with respect to profits attributable to a U.S. branch and not reinvested in that branch, paragraph 10 may apply to eliminate the branch profits tax if the company either met the publicly traded test, met both the ownership-base erosion and active trade or business tests, or met the derivative benefits test. If a German company did not meet any of those tests, but otherwise qualified for benefits under Article 28, then the branch profits tax would apply at a rate of 5 percent, unless the German company is granted benefits with respect to the elimination of the branch profits tax by the competent authority pursuant to paragraph 7 of Article 28.

Paragraph 11

Paragraph 11 defines a pension fund to mean a person that is organized under the laws of a Contracting State and that is established and maintained in that State primarily to administer or provide pensions or other similar remuneration (including social security payments, disability pensions and widow's pensions) or to earn income for the benefit of one or more such persons, and in the case of the United States, is exempt from tax in the United States with respect to such activities, or in the case of the Federal Republic of Germany, is a plan the contributions to which are eligible for preferential treatment under the Income Tax Act.

Relation to Other Articles

Notwithstanding the foregoing limitations on source country taxation of dividends, the saving clause of paragraph 4 of Article 1 (General Scope) permits the United States to tax dividends received by its residents and citizens, subject to the special foreign tax credit rules of paragraph 5 of Article 23 (Relief from Double Taxation), as if the Convention had not come into effect.

The benefits of this Article are also subject to the provisions of Article 28 (Limitation on Benefits). Thus, if a resident of the Federal Republic of Germany is the beneficial owner of dividends paid by a U.S. corporation, the shareholder must qualify for treaty benefits under at least one of the tests of Article 28 in order to receive the benefits of this Article.

Article V

Paragraph a) of Article V of the Protocol provides for a new paragraph 6 of Article 11 (Interest) of the Convention.   Paragraph 6 provides an anti-abuse exception to paragraph 1 of Article 11 (Interest) for excess inclusions from U.S. real estate mortgage investment conduits ("REMICs") that follows subparagraph (b) of paragraph 5 of the 1996 U.S. Model.   Paragraph 6 serves as a backstop to Code section 860G(b). That section generally requires that a foreign person holding a residual interest in a REMIC take into account for U.S. tax purposes "any excess inclusion" and "amounts includible . . . [under the REMIC provisions] when paid or distributed (or when the interest is disposed of) . . . ."

Without a full tax at source, non-U.S. transferees of residual interests would have a competitive advantage over U.S. transferees at the time these interests are initially offered. Absent this rule, the United States would suffer a revenue loss with respect to mortgages held in a REMIC because of opportunities for tax avoidance created by differences in the timing of taxable and economic income produced by such interests. In many cases, the transfer to the foreign person is simply disregarded under Reg. § 1.860G-3. Paragraph 6 also serves to indicate that excess inclusions from REMICs are not considered "other income" subject to Article 21 (Other Income) of the Convention.

Paragraph b) of Article V of the Protocol provides for an amended cross-reference in paragraph 5 of Article 11 (Interest) of the Convention.

Article VI

Article VI of the Protocol replaces the existing paragraph 6 of Article 13 (Gains) of the Convention. Paragraph 6 of Article 13 (Gains) provides special basis adjustment rules where an individual, who upon ceasing to be a resident of a Contracting State, is treated under the taxation laws of that State as having alienated property and is taxed in that State by reason thereof. Such an individual may elect to be treated for purposes of taxation in the other Contracting State as if the individual had, immediately before ceasing to be a resident of the first-mentioned Contracting State to have alienated and reacquired the property for amount equal to its fair market value. As a consequence of the election,, the other Contracting State, for purposes of imposing tax on any subsequent sale of the property, will be limited to the gain (if any) accrued once the individual ceased to be a resident of the first-mentioned Contracting State.

Notwithstanding the forgoing provisions, subparagraph (a) of paragraph 4 of the Article 1(General Scope) permits the United States to tax its citizens and residents as if the Convention had not come into effect. The rules of paragraph 6 of this Article, however, continue to apply to U.S. citizens and residents by virtue of the exceptions to the saving clause in subparagraph (a) of paragraph 5.

Article VII

Article VII of the Protocol deletes the existing Article 14 (Independent Personal Services) of the Convention. Accordingly, paragraph b) of Article III of the Protocol amends Article 7 (Business Profits) to provide that income from the performance of professional services and other activities of an independent character is included in the term business profits. This is consistent with recent U.S. tax treaty practice.

Article VIII

Article VIII of the Protocol changes the name Article 18 (Pensions, Annuities, Alimony, and Child Support) of the Convention to Article 18 (Pensions, Annuities, Alimony, Child Support, and Social Security).

In addition, Article VIII of the Protocol adds a new paragraph 5 to Article 18, the substance of which was previously contained in Article 19 (Government Service; Social Security). Paragraph 5 provides for exclusive residence-country taxation of social security benefits and similar public pensions. Paragraph 5 provides that payments made by one of the Contracting States under the provisions of its social security law and other public pensions (not dealt with in new Article 19 (Government Service)) to a resident of the other Contracting State will be taxable only in the other Contracting State. The phrase "other public pensions" is intended to refer to United States Tier 1 Railroad Retirement benefits. Paragraph 5 applies to social security beneficiaries, whether they have contributed to the system as private-sector or government employees. The treatment of social security benefits in the Convention differs from that in the U.S. Model which provides for exclusive source country taxation of social security benefits.

In applying its tax, the residence country will treat the benefit as though it were a benefit paid to a resident under its own social security system. Thus, for example, if a U.S. resident receives a German social security benefit, he would include only one half of the benefit or such other portion as he would if the benefit had been a U.S. social security or railroad retirement benefit.

With respect the Article 18, the Joint Declaration acknowledges that the Federal Republic of Germany has recently amended its domestic law regarding the taxation of retirement income and contributions to pension plans. However, these new rules are subject to a long phase-in period. Consequently, the Contracting States have agreed to enter into consultations no sooner than January 1, 2013 with a view to further amending this Article in light of this legislation.

Article IX

Article IX of the Protocol adds a new Article 18A (Pension Plans) to the Convention. Article 18A deals with cross-border pension contributions. It is intended to remove barriers to the flow of personal services between the Contracting States that could otherwise result from discontinuities in the laws of the Contracting States regarding the deductibility of pension contributions and the taxation of a pension plan's earnings and accretions. Such discontinuities may arise where countries allow deductions or exclusions to their residents for contributions, made by them or on their behalf, to resident pension plans, but do not allow deductions or exclusions for payments made to plans resident in another country, even if the structure and legal requirements of such plans in the two countries are similar. Similar discontinuities may arise where countries allow their residents to defer taxation on a pension plan's earnings and accretions, but do not allow such deferral for plans resident in another country.

The 2006 U.S. Model includes a comparable set of rules in Article 18 (Pension Funds).

Paragraph 1

Paragraph 1 provides that if a resident of a Contracting State participates in a pension plan established in the other Contracting State, the State of residence will not tax the income of the pension plan with respect to that resident until a distribution is made from the pension plan. Thus, for example, if a U.S. citizen contributes to a U.S. qualified plan while working in the United States and then establishes residence in the Federal Republic of Germany, paragraph 1 prevents the Federal Republic of Germany from taxing currently the plan's earnings and accretions with respect to that individual. When the resident receives a distribution from the pension plan, that distribution may be subject to tax in the State of residence, subject to paragraph 1 of Article 18 (Pensions, Annuities, Alimony, Child Support, and Social Security).

Paragraph 2

Paragraph 2 provides certain benefits with respect to cross-border contributions to a pension plan, subject to the limitations of paragraph 3 and 5 of the Article. It is irrelevant for purposes of paragraph 2 whether the participant establishes residence in the State where the individual renders services (the "host State"). The benefits provided in paragraph 2 are similar to the benefits the U.S. Model provides with respect to contributions.

Subparagraph (a) of paragraph 2 allows an individual who exercises employment or self-employment in a Contracting State to deduct or exclude from income in that Contracting State contributions made by or on behalf of the individual during the period of employment or self-employment to a pension plan established in the other Contracting State. Thus, for example, if a participant in a U.S. qualified plan goes to work in the Federal Republic of Germany, the participant may deduct or exclude from income in the

Federal Republic of Germany contributions to the U.S. qualified plan made while the participant works in the Federal Republic of Germany. Subparagraph (a), however, applies only to the extent of the relief allowed by the host State (*i.e.*, the Federal Republic of Germany in the example) to a resident of that State for contributions to a pension plan established in that State.

Subparagraph (b) of paragraph 2 provides that, in the case of employment, accrued benefits and contributions by or on behalf of the individual's employer, during the period of employment in the host State, will not be treated as taxable income to the employee in that State. Subparagraph (b) also allows the employer a deduction in computing business profits in the host State for contributions to the plan. For example, if a participant in a U.S. qualified plan goes to work in the Federal Republic of Germany, the participant's employer may deduct from its business profits in the Federal Republic of Germany contributions to the U.S. qualified plan for the benefit of the employee while the employee renders services in the Federal Republic of Germany.

As in the case of subparagraph (a), subparagraph (b) applies only to the extent of relief allowed by the host State to a resident of that State for contributions to, or benefits accrued under, a pension plan established in that State. Therefore, where the United States is the host State, the exclusion of employee contributions from the employee's income under this paragraph is limited to elective contributions not in excess of the amount specified in section 402(g). Deduction of employer contributions is subject to the limitations of sections 415 and 404. The section 404 limitation on deductions is calculated as if the individual were the only employee covered by the plan.

The competent authorities shall determine the relief available under subparagraphs (a) and (b) of paragraph 2.

Paragraph 3

Paragraph 3 limits the availability of benefits under paragraph 2. Under subparagraph (a) of paragraph 3, paragraph 2 does not apply to contributions to a pension plan unless the participant already was contributing to the plan, or his employer already was contributing to the plan with respect to that individual, before the individual began exercising employment in the host State. This condition would be met if either the employee or the employer was contributing to a plan that was replaced by the plan to which he is contributing. The rule regarding successor plans would apply if, for example, the employer has been taken over by a company that replaces the existing plan with its own plan, rolling membership in the old plan over into the new plan.

In addition, under subparagraph (b) of paragraph 3, the competent authority of the host State must determine that the recognized plan to which a contribution is made in the other Contracting State generally corresponds to the plan in the host State. Pursuant to clause (b)(aa) of paragraph 16 of Article XVI, the U.S. pension plans eligible for the benefits of paragraph 2 include the following plans (and any identical or substantially similar plans established pursuant to legislation enacted after the date of signature of this

Protocol): qualified plans under section 401(a) of the Internal Revenue Code, individual retirement plans (including individual retirement plans that are part of a simplified employee pension plan that satisfies section 408(k), individual retirement accounts, individual retirement annuities, and section 408(p) accounts), section 403(a) qualified annuity plans, section 403(b) plans, and section 457(b) governmental plans. Clause (b)(bb) of paragraph 16 of Article XVI provides that it is understood for this purpose that German plans include arrangements under section 1 of the German law on employment-related pensions (*Betriebsrentengesetz*).

Paragraph 4

Paragraph 4 defines the term "pension plan" for purposes of Article 18A to mean an arrangement established in a Contracting State which is operated principally to administer or provide pension or retirement benefits or to earn income for the benefit of one or more such arrangements. Clause (a)(aa) of paragraph 16 of Article XVI of the Protocol provides that the term "pension plan" shall include the following U.S. plans and any identical or substantially similar plans established pursuant to legislation enacted after the date of signature of this Protocol: qualified plans under section 401(a) of the Code, individual retirement plans (including individual retirement plans that are part of a simplified employee pension plan that satisfies section 408(k), individual retirement accounts, individual retirement annuities, and section 408(p) accounts, and Roth IRAs under Section 408A), section 403(a) qualified annuity plans, section 403(b) plans, and section 457(b) governmental plans. In the case of the Federal Republic of Germany, clause (a)(bb) of paragraph 16 of Article XVI of the Protocol provides that the term "pension plan" shall include arrangements under section 1 of the German law on employment related pensions (*Betriebsrentengesetz*) and any identical or substantially similar plans established pursuant to legislation enacted after the date of signature of this Protocol.

Paragraph 5

Paragraph 5 generally provides U.S. tax treatment for certain contributions by or on behalf of U.S. citizens resident in the Federal Republic of Germany to pension plans established in the Federal Republic of Germany that is comparable to the treatment that would be provided for contributions to U.S. plans. Under clause (aa) of subparagraph (a) of paragraph 5, a U.S. citizen resident in the Federal Republic of Germany may exclude or deduct for U.S. tax purposes certain contributions to a pension plan established in the Federal Republic of Germany. Qualifying contributions generally include contributions made during the period the U.S. citizen exercises an employment in the Federal Republic of Germany the income from which is taxable in the Federal Republic if expenses of the employment are borne by a German employer or German permanent establishment. Similarly, with respect to the U.S. citizen's participation in the German pension plan, accrued benefits and contributions during that period generally are not treated as taxable income in the United States under clause (bb) of subparagraph (a) of paragraph 5.

The U.S. tax benefit allowed by paragraph 5, however, is limited to the lesser of the amount of relief allowed for contributions and benefits under a pension plan established in the Federal Republic of Germany and, under subparagraph (b), the amount of relief that would be allowed for contributions and benefits under a generally corresponding pension plan established in the United States.

Subparagraph (c) provides that the benefits an individual obtains under paragraph 5 are counted when determining that individual's eligibility for benefits under a pension plan established in the United States. Thus, for example, contributions to a German pension plan may be counted in determining whether the individual has exceeded the annual limitation on contributions to an individual retirement account.

Under subparagraph (d), paragraph 5 does not apply to pension contributions and benefits unless the competent authority of the United States has agreed that the pension plan established in the Federal Republic of Germany generally corresponds to a pension plan established in the United States. Paragraph 16 of Article XIV provides that certain pension plans have been determined to "generally correspond" to plans in the other country. Since paragraph 5 applies only with respect to persons employed by a German employer or German permanent establishment, however, the relevant German plans are those that correspond to employer plans in the United States. Accordingly, it applies with respect to retirement benefit plans under section 1 of the German law on employment related pensions (*Betriebsrentengesetz*).

Relation to other Articles

Paragraphs 1 and 5 are not subject to the saving clause of paragraph 4 of Article 1 (General Scope) by reason of the exception in subparagraph 5(a) of Article 1. Thus, the United States will allow U.S. citizens and residents the benefits of paragraphs 1 and 5. Paragraph 2 is not subject to the saving clause by reason of subparagraph 5(b) of Article 1. Accordingly, a person who becomes a U.S. permanent resident or citizen will no longer receive a deduction for contributions to a pension fund established in the other Contracting State.

Article X

Article X of the Protocol replaces Article 19 (Government Services) of the Convention. The amendments made by this Article X of the Protocol will not have effect with respect to individuals who, at the time of the signing of the Convention, August 29, 1989, were employed by the United States, a political subdivision or local authority thereof.

Paragraph 1

Subparagraphs (a) and (b) of paragraph 1 deal with the taxation of government compensation (other than a pension addressed in paragraph 2). Subparagraph (a) provides that salaries, wages and other similar remuneration paid to any individual who is rendering services to that State, political subdivision, local authority, or instrumentality is exempt from tax by the other State (*i.e.*, the host State). Under subparagraph (b), such payments are, however, taxable exclusively in the host State if the services are rendered in the host State and the individual is a resident of that State who is either a national of that State or a person who did not become resident of that State solely for purposes of rendering the services.

This paragraph follows the OECD Model, but differs from the U.S. Model in applying only to government employees and not to independent contractors engaged by governments to perform services for them.

Paragraph 2

Paragraph 2 deals with the taxation of pensions and other similar remuneration paid by, or out of funds created by, one of the States, or a political subdivision, local authority, or instrumentality thereof, to an individual in respect of services rendered to that State, subdivision, authority or instrumentality. Subparagraph (a) provides that such pensions and other remuneration are taxable only in that State. Subparagraph (b) provides an exception under which such pensions are taxable only in the other State if the individual is a resident of, and a national of, that other State or the pension is not subject to tax in the Contracting State for which the services were performed because the services were performed entirely in the other Contracting State.

Pensions paid to retired civilian and military employees of a Government of either State are intended to be covered under paragraph 2. When benefits paid by a State in respect of services rendered to that State (or a subdivision, authority, or instrumentality) are in the form of social security benefits, however, those payments are covered by paragraph 5 of Article 18 (Pensions, Annuities, Alimony, Child Support, and Social Security). The result will differ depending upon whether Article 18 or 19 applies, since social security benefits are generally taxable exclusively by the residence country while government pensions are generally taxable exclusively by the source country.

Paragraph 3

Paragraph 3 contains a provision proposed by the Federal Republic of Germany. It is based on a provision in the 1954 Convention. The subparagraph provides that pension, annuities, and other amounts paid by a Contracting State or by a juridical person organized under the public laws of that State that are compensation for injury or damage sustained as a result of hostilities or political persecution are exempt from tax in the other Contracting State. Although the subparagraph is drafted reciprocally, it is intended to provide an exemption from U.S. tax for German war reparation payments.

Paragraph 4

Paragraph 4 specifies that paragraphs 1 and 2 do not apply to salaries, wages, or similar remuneration, and to pensions, paid for services performed in connection with a business carried on by a Contracting State, or a political subdivision, local authority or instrumentality thereof. In such cases, the remuneration and pensions are subject instead to the provisions of Articles 15 (Dependant Personal Services), 16 (Directors' Fees), or 17 (Artistes and Athletes) and 18 (Pensions, Annuities, Alimony, Child Support, and Social Security). This provision conforms to the OECD Model.

Paragraph 5

For purposes of this Article, the term "instrumentality" means an agent or entity created or organized by a Contracting State, one of its states or a political subdivision or local authority thereof in order to carry out functions of a government nature which is specified and agreed to in letters exchanged between the competent authorities of the Contracting States.

Relation to other Articles

Under subparagraph (b) of paragraph 5 of Article 1 (General Scope), the saving clause (paragraph 4 of Article 1) does not apply to the benefits conferred if the recipient of the benefits is neither a citizen of United States, nor a person who has been admitted for permanent residence there (*i.e.*, a "green card" holder). Thus, for example, a resident of the Federal Republic of Germany who, in the course of rendering services to the government of the Federal Republic of Germany, becomes a resident of the United States (but not a permanent resident) would be entitled to the exemption from taxation by the United States provided by paragraph 1. However, Article 19 is subject to the saving clause with respect to benefits conferred by the United States to citizens and permanent residents of the United States.

Paragraph 3 of this Article is an exception to the saving clause (paragraph 4 of Article 1) pursuant to subparagraph (a) of paragraph 5 of Article 1(General Scope). Thus, a U.S. citizen or resident who receives German reparations payments would not be subject to any U.S. tax on that payment, regardless of whether he would be taxable under the Code.

Article XI

Paragraph (a) of Article XI of the Protocol replaces paragraph 1 of Article 20 (Visiting Professors and Teachers; Students and Trainees). Paragraph 1 provides that a professor or teacher who is resident in one Contracting State and who is temporarily present in the other Contracting State for the primary purpose of carrying out advanced study or research, or for teaching at a recognized educational institution, or an institution engaged in research for the public benefit in that other State will be exempted from tax by that other State on any remuneration for such teaching or research for a period not exceeding two years from the date he first visits that other State for the purpose of advanced study, teaching, or research. Since this two year period is determined from the date he first visits the other State, periodic vacations outside the other State, or a brief return to the first-mentioned State will not toll the running of the two-year period. Unlike the existing Convention, if the two-year period beginning from the date of his arrival is exceeded, the exemption will apply, but only for the first two years and only if the visit is temporary. Thus, if a person comes to a Contracting State for the purpose of teaching and stays for a temporary period in excess of two years, the person will not retroactively lose the exemption with respect to the first two years. The professor or teacher will not be granted the benefits of this provision if, during the period immediately preceding his visit, he enjoyed the benefits of paragraph 2, 3, or 4 of this Article or he was not a resident of the first-mentioned State.

A person who meets the qualifications for this exemption may again claim its benefits if he first re-establishes his residence in the other Contracting State. In such case, the person claiming these benefits on a subsequent occasion must first satisfy the competent authority of the first-mentioned Contracting State that he had become a resident of the other State for a substantial period of time (normally at least one year).

Article XII

Article XII of the Protocol replaces Article 23 (Relief from Double Taxation) of the Convention. Article 23 of the Convention addresses the manner in which each Contracting State undertakes to relieve double taxation. The United States uses the foreign tax credit method under its internal law and by treaty. The Federal Republic of Germany uses a combination of the foreign tax credit and exemption methods, depending on the nature of the income involved.

Paragraph 1

The United States agrees, in subparagraph (a) of paragraph 1, to allow to its citizens and residents a credit against U.S. tax for income taxes paid or accrued to the Federal Republic of Germany. For this purpose, the taxes covered by subparagraph (b) of paragraph 1 and by paragraph 2 of Article 2 (Taxes Covered), other than the capital tax (*Vermoegensteuer*) are income taxes. Thus, the German income tax (*Einkommensteurer)*, the corporate income tax (*Koerperschaftsteuer*), the trade tax (*Gewerbesteuer*), as well as any identical or substantially similar German taxes that are imposed after the date of signature of the Convention in addition to, or in place of, these existing taxes, are considered to be income taxes for purposes of paragraph 1. The granting of a foreign tax credit with respect to German taxes is based on the Treasury Department's review of the laws of the Federal Republic of Germany.

Subparagraph (b) provides for a deemed-paid credit, consistent with section 902 of the Code to a U.S. corporation in respect of dividends received from a corporation resident in the Federal Republic of Germany of which the U.S. corporation owns at least 10 percent of the voting stock. This credit is for the tax paid by the German corporation on the profits out of which the dividends are considered paid.

The credits allowed under paragraph 1 are allowed in accordance with the provisions and subject to the limitations of U.S. law, as that law may be amended over time, so long as the general principle of the Article, that is, the allowance of a credit, is retained. Thus, although the Convention provides for a foreign tax credit, the terms of the credit are determined by the provisions, at the time a credit is given, of the U.S. statutory credit.

Therefore, the U.S. credit under the Convention is subject to the various limitations of U.S. law (see Code sections 901-908). For example, the credit against U.S. tax generally is limited to the amount of U.S. tax due with respect to net foreign source income within the relevant foreign tax credit limitation category (see Code section 904(a) and (d)), and the dollar amount of the credit is determined in accordance with U.S. currency translation rules (*see, e.g.,* Code section 986). Similarly, U.S. law applies to determine carryover periods for excess credits and other inter-year adjustments.

Paragraph 2

Paragraph 2 provides a re-sourcing rule for gross income covered by paragraph 1. Paragraph 2 is intended to ensure that a U.S. resident can obtain a U.S. foreign tax credit for German taxes paid when the Convention assigns to the Federal Republic of Germany primary taxing rights over an item of gross income.

Paragraph 2 provides that, if the Convention allows the Federal Republic of Germany to tax an item of gross income (as defined under U.S. law) derived by a resident of the United States, the United States will treat that item of gross income as gross income from sources within the Federal Republic of Germany for U.S. foreign tax credit purposes. In the case of a U.S.-owned foreign corporation, however, section 904(h)(10) may apply for purposes of determining the U.S. foreign tax credit with respect to income subject to this re-sourcing rule. Section 904(h)(10) generally applies the foreign tax credit limitation separately to re-sourced income. Furthermore, the paragraph 2 re-sourcing rule applies to gross income, not net income. Accordingly, U.S. expense allocation and apportionment rules, *see, e.g.,* Treas. Reg. section 1.861-9, continue to apply to income resourced under paragraph 2.

Paragraph 3

Paragraph 3 provides that the Federal Republic of Germany will relieve double taxation on German residents through a dual method of exemption and credit. Subparagraph (a) of paragraph 3 generally provides an exemption from the German tax base for income or capital that may be taxed in the United States under the Convention or that is exempt from U.S. tax under Article 10(3) (except in cases where a foreign tax credit is provided for under subparagraph (b) of paragraph 3). However, the Federal Republic of Germany may take the excluded income and assets into account in determining the rate of tax on other items of income and capital (i.e., the Federal Republic of Germany may provide for exemption with progression).

Subparagraph (a) of paragraph 3 also provides that in the case of German resident companies (not including partnerships) that own at least 10 percent of the voting shares of U.S. resident companies, the Federal Republic of Germany will only exempt distributions of profits on corporate rights subject to corporate income tax under U.S. law. In addition, the exemption shall not apply to dividends from a RIC or REIT and distributions that are deductible for U.S. income tax purposes by the distributing company. With respect to German capital taxes, the Federal Republic of Germany will exclude any shareholding the dividends on which would be exempt from German income tax under subparagraph (a) of paragraph 3.

The principal types of income for which exemption is allowed under subparagraph (a) of paragraph 3 are generally: (i) income derived by a German enterprise which is attributable to a permanent establishment in the United States, (ii) many kinds of capital gains, (iii) most classes of personal services income, and (iv) dividends from direct investments in the United States.

Subparagraph (b) of paragraph 2 indicates those items of income, which have been taxed in the United States in accordance with the provisions of U.S. law and the Convention, for which the Federal Republic of Germany will provide a foreign tax credit rather than exemption. These are: (i) income from dividends (as defined in Article 10 (Dividends)) for which the Federal Republic of Germany will not grant exemption under subparagraph (a) of paragraph 3 of this Article (e.g., portfolio dividends, RIC dividends and similar deductible or pass-through entity dividends); (ii) gains from the alienation of immovable property to which Article 13 (Gains) apply provided such gains are taxable in the United States by reason only of paragraph 2 of Article 13 (Gains); (iii) income to which Article 16 (Directors' Fees) applies received by German residents in respect of their services rendered in the United States as directors of U.S. corporations, (iv) income to which Article 17 (Artistes and Athletes) applies, (v) income which would be exempt from U.S. tax under the Convention (e.g., interest), but which is denied the benefits of the Convention and is subject to tax by virtue of Article 28 (Limitation on Benefits). With respect to (v) above, such income would be fully taxable in the Federal Republic of Germany with no credit for U.S. tax absent a special provision; the provision provides for a German foreign tax credit in cases where the United States taxes solely by virtue of the Limitation on Benefits provisions.

As with the U.S. credit under paragraph 1, the foreign tax credit granted by the Federal Republic of Germany under the Convention is subject to the provisions of German law regarding a credit for foreign taxes. Income that may be taxed in the United States in accordance with the Convention is deemed, for purposes of the German foreign tax credit and exemption provided in paragraph 3, to be from U.S. sources.

Paragraph 4

The Federal Republic of Germany will provide a foreign tax credit pursuant to subparagraph (b) of paragraph 3 (as opposed to exemption under subparagraph (a) of paragraph 3) in three additional instances. The change from the exemption method to credit method provided by this paragraph is designed to prevent unintended instances either of double taxation or of double non-taxation or inappropriately low taxation.

First, the Federal Republic of Germany provides a foreign tax credit if income or capital would be subject to double taxation as a result of the placement of such income under different provisions of the Convention and this conflict cannot be resolved pursuant to Article 25 (Mutual Agreement Procedure).

Second, the Federal Republic of Germany will provide a foreign tax credit on income or capital if the United States applies the provisions of the Convention to exempt such income or capital from tax, or applies paragraph 2 or 3 of Article 10 (Dividends) to such income or capital or may under the provisions of the Convention tax such income or capital but is prevented from doing so under its domestic law.

Third, the Federal Republic of Germany may switch from an exemption to a foreign tax credit for items of income or capital to the extent consistent with internal German law and, after due consultation with the United States and notification of the United States through diplomatic channels (switchover clause). In such a case, the provisions of subparagraph b) of paragraph 3 shall apply for all taxable years following the year of such notification. Any changes in treatment or characterization that may be made pursuant to subparagraph c) of paragraph 4 can be effective only from the beginning of the calendar year following the year in which the formal notification of the change was transmitted to the United States and only when any legal prerequisites for the change in the domestic law of the Federal Republic of Germany have been fulfilled.

The so-called "switchover clause" is intended to deal with cases of double exemption of income (e.g., through the granting of a dividends paid deduction to the U.S. payor of a dividend and a correlative exemption of such dividend in Germany) or arrangements for improper use of the Convention. It was not intended to apply to cases where the profits out of which a distribution is made have been subject to the general U.S. corporate-level taxing regime. Thus, for example, the fact that a U.S. corporation pays a reduced level of U.S. corporate-level tax because of the nature or source of its income (e.g., because it is entitled to a dividends received deduction, a net operating loss carry forward, or a foreign tax credit) will not entitle Germany to switch from exemption to credit.

Paragraph 5

Paragraph 5 provides special rules for the tax treatment in both Contracting States of certain types of income derived from U.S. sources by U.S. citizens who are resident in the Federal Republic of Germany. Since U.S. citizens, regardless of residence, are subject to United States tax at ordinary progressive rates on their worldwide income, the U.S. tax on the U.S. source income of a U.S. citizen resident in the Federal Republic of Germany may exceed the U.S. tax that may be imposed under the Convention on an item of U.S. source income derived by a resident of the Federal Republic of Germany who is not a U.S. citizen. The provisions of paragraph 5 ensure that the Federal Republic of Germany does not bear the cost of U.S. taxation of its citizens who are German residents.

Subparagraph (a) provides, with respect to items of income from sources within the United States, special German credit rules. These rules apply to items of U.S.-source income that would be either exempt from U.S. tax or subject to reduced rates of U.S. tax under the provisions of the Convention if they had been received by a German resident who is not a U.S. citizen. The tax credit allowed under paragraph 5 with respect to such items need not exceed the U.S. tax that may be imposed under the Convention, other than tax imposed solely by reason of the U.S. citizenship of the taxpayer under the provisions of the saving clause of paragraph 4 of Article 1 (General Scope).

For example, if a U.S. citizen resident in Germany receives portfolio dividends from sources within the United States, the German foreign tax credit would be limited to 15 percent of the dividend - - the U.S. tax that may be imposed under subparagraph 2(b) of Article 10 (Dividends) - - even if the shareholder is subject (before the special U.S. foreign tax credit and source rules provided for in subparagraphs 5(b) and 5(c)) to U.S. net income tax because of his U.S. citizenship as a result of the saving clause. With respect to royalty or interest income, Germany would allow no foreign tax credit, because German residents are exempt from U.S. tax on these classes of income under the provisions of Articles 11 (Interest) and 12 (Royalties).

Subparagraph 5(b) eliminates the potential for double taxation that can arise as a result of the absence of a full German foreign tax credit, because of subparagraph 5a), for the U.S. tax imposed on its citizens who are German residents. The subparagraph provides that the United States will credit the German income tax paid or accrued, after the application of subparagraph 5a). It further provides that in allowing the credit, the United States will not reduce its tax below the amount which is allowed as a creditable tax in Germany under subparagraph 5a).

Since the income described in paragraph 5(a) generally will be U.S. source income, special rules are required to resource some of the income as German source in order for the United States to be able to credit the German tax. This resourcing is provided for in subparagraph 5c), which deems the items of income referred to in subparagraph 5a) to be from German sources to the extent necessary to avoid double taxation under subparagraph 5b). Subparagraph 3(c)(cc) of Article 25 (Mutual Agreement Procedure) provides a mechanism by which the competent authorities can resolve any disputes regarding whether income is from sources within the United States.

The following two examples illustrate the application of paragraph 5 in the case of a U.S.-source portfolio dividend received by a U.S. citizen resident in the Federal Republic of Germany. In both examples, the U.S. rate of tax on residents of the Federal Republic of Germany, under subparagraph (b) of paragraph 2 of Article 10 (Dividends) of the Convention, is 15 percent. In both examples, the U.S. income tax rate on the U.S. citizen is 35 percent. In example 1, the German income tax rate on its resident (the U.S. citizen) is 25 percent (below the U.S. rate), and in example 2, the German rate on its resident is 40 percent (above the U.S. rate).

	Example 1	Example 2
Subparagraph (a)		
U.S. dividend declared	$100.00	$100.00
Notional U.S. withholding tax (Article 10(2)(b))	15.00	15.00
German taxable income	100.00	100.00
German tax before credit	25.00	40.00
German foreign tax credit for notional U.S. withholding tax	15.00	15.00
Net post-credit German tax	10.00	25.00
Subparagraphs (b) and (c)		
U.S. pre-tax income	$100.00	$100.00
U.S. pre-credit citizenship tax	35.00	35.00
Notional U.S. withholding tax	15.00	15.00
U.S. tax available for credit	20.00	20.00
Tax paid to other Contracting State	10.00	25.00
Income re-sourced from U.S. to German (see below)	28.57	57.14
U.S. pre-credit tax on re-sourced income	10.00	20.00
U.S. credit for German tax	10.00	20.00
Net post-credit U.S. tax	10.00	0.00
Total U.S. tax	25.00	15.00

In both examples, in the application of subparagraph (a), the Federal Republic of Germany credits a 15 percent U.S. tax against its residence tax on the U.S. citizen. In the first example, the net German tax after the German foreign tax credit is $10.00; in the second example, it is $25.00. In the application of subparagraphs (b) and (c), from the U.S. tax due before credit of $35.00, the United States subtracts the amount of the U.S. source tax of $15.00, against which no U.S. foreign tax credit is allowed. This subtraction ensures that the United States collects the tax that it is due under the Convention as the State of source.

In both examples, given the 35 percent U.S. tax rate, the maximum amount of U.S. tax against which credit for the German tax may be claimed is $20 ($35 U.S. tax minus $15 U.S. withholding tax). Initially, all of the income in both examples was from sources within the United States. For a U.S. foreign tax credit to be allowed for the full amount of the German tax, an appropriate amount of the income must be re-sourced to the Federal Republic of Germany under subparagraph (c).

The amount that must be re-sourced depends on the amount of German tax for which the U.S. citizen is claiming a U.S. foreign tax credit. In example 1, the German tax was $10. For this amount to be creditable against U.S. tax, $28.57 ($10 German tax divided by 35 percent U.S. tax rate) must be resourced to the Federal Republic of Germany. When the German tax is credited against the $10 of U.S. tax on this resourced income, there is a net U.S. tax of $10 due after credit ($20 U.S. tax minus $10 German tax). Thus, in example 1, there is a total of $25 in U.S. tax ($15 U.S. withholding tax plus $10 residual U.S. tax).

In example 2, the German tax was $25, but, because the United States subtracts the U.S. withholding tax of $15 from the total U.S. tax of $35, only $20 of U.S. taxes may be offset by German taxes. Accordingly, the amount that must be resourced to the Federal Republic of Germany is limited to the amount necessary to ensure a U.S. foreign tax credit for $20 of German tax, or $57.14 ($20 German tax divided by 35 percent U.S. tax rate). When the German tax is credited against the U.S. tax on this re-sourced income, there is no residual U.S. tax ($20 U.S. tax minus $25 German tax, subject to the U.S. limit of $20). Thus, in example 2, there is a total of $15 in U.S. tax ($15 U.S. withholding tax plus $0 residual U.S. tax). Because the German tax was $25 and the U.S. tax available for credit was $20, there is $5 of excess U.S. tax credit available for carryover.

Relation to other articles

By virtue of subparagraph (a) of paragraph 5 of Article 1 (General Scope), Article 23 is not subject to the saving clause of paragraph 4 of Article 1. Thus, the United States will allow a credit to its citizens and residents in accordance with the Article, even if such credit were to provide a benefit not available under the Code (such as the re-sourcing provided by paragraph 2 and subparagraph 5(c)).

Article XIII

Article XIII of the Protocol deletes paragraph 5 of Article 25 (Mutual Agreement Procedure) of the Convention, providing for voluntary binding arbitration, and replaces it with new paragraphs 5 and 6, which introduce a mandatory binding arbitration procedure.

A case shall be resolved through arbitration when the competent authorities have endeavored but are unable to reach a complete agreement regarding a case through negotiation and the following three conditions are satisfied. First, tax returns have been filed with at least one of the Contracting States with respect to the taxable years at issue in the case. Second, the case: (i) is a case that involves one or more enumerated articles of the Convention, and is not a case that the competent authorities agree before the date on which arbitration proceedings would otherwise have begun, is not suitable for determination by arbitration; or (ii) is a case that the competent authorities agree is suitable for determination by arbitration. Third, all concerned persons and their authorized representatives agree not to disclose to any other person any information received during the course of the arbitration proceeding from either the Contracting States or the arbitration board, other than the determination of the board (confidentiality agreement). The confidentiality agreement may also be executed by any concerned person that has the legal authority to bind any other concerned person on the matter. For example, a parent corporation with the legal authority to bind its subsidiary with respect to confidentiality may execute a comprehensive confidentiality agreement on its own behalf and that of its subsidiary.

Paragraph 22 of Article XVI of the Protocol provides that cases regarding the application of one or more of the following articles may be the subject of mandatory binding arbitration, if the requirements of paragraphs 5 and 6 of Article 25 are otherwise satisfied: Article 4 (Residence) as its relates to residence of a natural person, Article 5 (Permanent Establishment), Article 7 (Business Profits), Article 9 (Associated Enterprises), and Article 12 (Royalties). The application of one or more of the other provisions in the Convention to which Article 25 applies may be the subject of binding arbitration should the competent authorities agree.

A concerned person means the person that brought the case to competent authority for consideration under Article 25 and includes all other persons, if any, whose tax liability to either Contracting State may be directly affected by a mutual agreement arising from that consideration. For example, a concerned person does not only include a U.S. corporation that brings a transfer pricing case with respect to a transaction entered into with its German subsidiary for resolution to the U.S. competent authority, but also the German subsidiary, which may have a correlative adjustment as a result of the resolution of the case.

An arbitration proceeding begins on the later of two dates: two years from the commencement date of that case, unless both competent authorities have previously agreed to a different date, or the earliest date upon which the all concerned persons have entered into a confidentiality agreement and the agreements have been received by both competent authorities. The commencement date is the earliest date on which information necessary to undertake substantive consideration for mutual agreement has been received by both competent authorities. Clause p) of paragraph 22 of Article XVI of the Protocol provides that each competent authority will confirm in writing to the other competent authority and to the concerned persons the date of its receipt of the information necessary to undertake substantive consideration for a mutual agreement. In the case of the United States, this information is (i) the information that must be submitted to the U.S. competent authority under Section 4.05 of Rev. Proc. 2002-52, 2002-2 C.B. 242, as it might be amended from time to time, and (ii) for cases initially submitted as a request for an Advance Pricing Agreement, the information that must be submitted to the Internal Revenue Service under Section 4 Rev. Proc. 2006-9, 2006-2 I.R.B. 278, as it might be amended from time to time. In the case of the Federal Republic of Germany, this information is the information that must be submitted to the German competent authority pursuant to the German Ministry of Finance's circular of July 1, 1997, -IV C 5 - S 1300 – 189/96. The information will not be considered received until both competent authorities receive copies of all materials submitted by concerned persons in connection with the mutual agreement procedure.

Paragraph 22 of Article XVI of the Protocol provides for a several procedural rules once an arbitration proceeding under paragraph 5 of Article 25 ("Proceeding") has commenced, but the competent authorities may modify or supplement these rules as necessary. In addition, the arbitration board may adopt any procedures necessary for the conduct of its business, provided the procedures are not inconsistent with any provision of Article 25 of the Convention.

Subparagraph (e) of paragraph 22 of Article XVI of the Protocol provides that each Contracting State has 60 days from the date on which the Proceeding begins to send a written communication to the other Contracting State appointing one member of the arbitration board. Within 60 days of the date the second of such communications is sent, these two board members will appoint a third member to serve as the chair of the board. The chair may not be a citizen of either Contracting State. In the event that any members of the board are not appointed (including as a result of the failure of the two members appointed by the Contracting States to agree on a third member) by the requisite date, the remaining members are appointed by the highest ranking member of the Secretariat at the Centre for Tax Policy and Administration of the Organisation for Economic Co-operation and Development (OECD) who is not a citizen of either Contracting State, by written notice to both Contracting States within 60 days of the date of such failure.

Clause (g) of paragraph 22 of Article XVI of the Protocol establishes deadlines for submission of materials by the Contracting States to the arbitration board. Each competent authority has 90 days from the date of appointment of the chair to submit a Proposed Resolution describing the proposed disposition of the specific monetary amounts of income, expense or taxation at issue in the case, and a supporting Position Paper. Copies of each State's submissions are to be provided by the board to the other Contracting State on the date the later of the submissions is submitted to the board. Each of the Contracting States may submit a Reply Submission to the board within 180 days of the appointment of the chair to address points raised in the other State's Proposed Resolution or Position Paper. If one Contracting State fails to submit a Proposed Resolution within the requisite time, the Proposed Resolution of the other Contracting State is deemed to be the determination of the arbitration board. No other information may be supplied to the arbitration board, unless it requests additional information. Copies of any such requested information, along with the board's request, must be provided to the other Contracting State on the date the request or response is submitted.

All communication with the board is to be in writing between the chair of the board and the designated competent authorities with the exception of communication regarding logistical matters.

In making its determination the arbitration board will apply the following authorities as necessary and in descending order of relevance: (i) the provisions of the Convention, (ii) any agreed commentaries or explanation of the Contracting States concerning the Convention, (iii) the laws of the Contracting States to the extent they are not inconsistent with each other, and (iv) any OECD Commentary, Guidelines or Reports regarding relevant analogous portions of the OECD Model Tax Convention.

The arbitration board must deliver a determination in writing to the Contracting States within 9 months of the appointment of the chair. The determination must be one of the two Proposed Resolutions submitted by the Contracting States. The determination may only provide a determination regarding the amount of income, expense or tax reportable to the Contracting States. The determination has no precedential value and consequently the rationale behind a board's determination would not be beneficial and may not be provided by the board.

Unless any concerned person does not accept the decision of the arbitration board, the determination of the board constitutes a resolution by mutual agreement under Article 25 and, consequently, is binding on both Contracting States. Within 30 days of receiving the determination from the competent authority to which the case was first presented, each concerned person must advise that competent authority whether the person accepts the determination. The failure to advise the competent authority within the requisite time is considered a rejection of the determination. In addition, if the case is in litigation, the concerned persons must advise the relevant court of their acceptance of the arbitration determination, and withdraw from the litigation the issues resolved by the MAP arbitration. If a determination is rejected the case cannot be the subject of a subsequent Proceeding. After the commencement of the Proceeding but before a decision of the board has been accepted by all concerned persons, the competent authorities may reach a mutual agreement to resolve the case and terminate the Proceeding.

For purposes of the arbitration proceeding, the members of the arbitration board and their staffs shall be considered "persons or authorities" to whom information may be disclosed under Article 26 (Exchange of Information and Administrative Assistance). Paragraph 22 of Article XVI of the Protocol provides that all materials prepared in the course of, or relating to the Proceeding are considered information exchanged between the Contracting States. No information relating to the Proceeding or the board's determination may be disclosed by members of the arbitration board or their staffs or by either competent authority, except as permitted by the Convention and the domestic laws of the Contracting States. Members of the arbitration board and their staffs must agree in statements sent to each of the Contracting States in confirmation of their appointment to the arbitration board to abide by and be subject to the confidentiality and nondisclosure provisions of Article 26 of the Convention and the applicable domestic laws of the Contracting States, with the most restrictive of the provisions applying.

The applicable domestic law of the Contracting States determines the treatment of any interest or penalties associated with a competent authority agreement achieved through arbitration.

Fees and expenses are borne equally by the Contracting States, including the cost of translation services. In general, the fees of members of the arbitration board will be set at the fixed amount of $2,000 per day (or the equivalent amount in Euro). The expenses of members of the board will be set in accordance with the International Centre for Settlement of Investment Disputes (ICSID) Schedule of Fees for arbitrators (in effect on the date on which the arbitration board proceedings begin). The competent authorities may amend the set fees and expenses of members of the board. Meeting facilities, related resources, financial management, other logistical support, and general and administrative coordination of the Proceeding will be provided, at its own cost, by the Contracting State whose competent authority initiated the mutual agreement proceedings. All other costs are to be borne by the Contracting State that incurs them.

Article XIV

Article XIV of the Protocol replaces Article 28 (Limitation on Benefits) of the Convention.

Structure of the Article

Article 28 contains anti-treaty-shopping provisions that are intended to prevent residents of third countries from benefiting from what is intended to be a reciprocal agreement between two countries. In general, the provision does not rely on a determination of purpose or intention but instead sets forth a series of objective tests. A resident of a Contracting State that satisfies one of the tests will receive benefits regardless of its motivations in choosing its particular business structure.

The structure of the Article is as follows: Paragraph 1 states the general rule that a resident of a Contracting State is entitled to benefits otherwise accorded to residents only to the extent that the resident is a "qualified person" and satisfies any satisfies any other conditions specified in the Convention for the obtaining of benefits. Paragraph 2 lists a series of attributes of a resident of a Contracting State, any one of which suffices to make such resident a "qualified person" and thus entitled to all the benefits of the Convention. Paragraph 3 provides a so-called "derivative benefits" test under which certain categories of income may qualify for benefits. Paragraph 4 sets forth the "active trade or business test", under which a person may be granted benefits with regard to certain types of income regardless of whether the person is a qualified person. Paragraph 5 provides special rules for so-called "triangular cases" notwithstanding the other provisions of Article 28. Paragraph 6 provides a special rule for *Investmentvermögen*. Paragraph 7 provides that benefits may also be granted if the competent authority of the State from which the benefits are claimed determines that it is appropriate to grant benefits in that case. Paragraph 8 defines the terms used specifically in this Article.

Paragraph 1

Paragraph 1 provides that, except as otherwise provided, a resident of a Contracting State is entitled to all the benefits of the Convention otherwise accorded to residents of a Contracting State only if the resident is a "qualified person" as defined in paragraph 2 of Article 28.

The benefits otherwise accorded to residents under the Convention include all limitations on source-based taxation under Articles 6 through 22, the treaty-based relief from double taxation, and the protection afforded to residents of a Contracting State under Article 24 (Nondiscrimination). Some provisions do not require that a person be a resident in order to enjoy the benefits of those provisions. For example, Article 25 (Mutual Agreement Procedure) is not limited to residents of the Contracting States, and Article 19 (Government Service) applies to government employees regardless of residence. Article 28 accordingly does not limit the availability of treaty benefits under such provisions.

Article 28 and the anti-abuse provisions of domestic law complement each other, as Article 28 effectively determines whether an entity has a sufficient nexus to a Contracting State to be treated as a resident for treaty purposes, while domestic anti-abuse provisions (e.g., business purpose, substance-over-form, step transaction or conduit principles) determine whether a particular transaction should be recast in accordance with its substance. Thus, internal law principles of the source Contracting State may be applied to identify the beneficial owner of an item of income, and Article 28 then will be applied to the beneficial owner to determine if that person is entitled to the benefits of the Convention with respect to such income.

Paragraph 2

Paragraph 2 has six subparagraphs, each of which describes a category of residents that are entitled to all benefits of the Convention. It is intended that the provisions of paragraph 2 will be self-executing. Claiming benefits under paragraph 2 does not require an advance competent authority ruling or approval. The tax authorities may, of course, on review, determine that the taxpayer has improperly interpreted the paragraph and is not entitled to the benefits claimed.

Individuals -- Subparagraph 2(a)

Subparagraph (a) provides that individual residents of a Contracting State will be entitled to all the benefits of the Convention. If such an individual receives income as a nominee on behalf of a third country resident, benefits may be denied under the applicable articles of the Convention by the requirement that the beneficial owner of the income be a resident of a Contracting State.

Governments -- Subparagraph 2(b)

Subparagraph (b) provides that the Contracting States and any political subdivision or local authority thereof will be entitled to all the benefits of the Convention.

Publicly-Traded Corporations -- Subparagraph 2(c)(aa)

Subparagraph (c) applies to two categories of companies: publicly traded companies and subsidiaries of publicly traded companies. A company resident in a Contracting State is entitled to all the benefits of the Convention under clause (aa) of subparagraph (c) if the principal class of its shares, and any disproportionate class of shares, is regularly traded on one or more recognized stock exchanges and the company satisfies at least one of the following additional tests. First, the company's principal class of shares is primarily traded on a recognized stock exchange located in a Contracting State of which the company is a resident. Second, the company's primary place of management and control is in its State of residence.

The term "recognized stock exchange" is defined in subparagraph (a) of paragraph 8. It includes the NASDAQ System and any stock exchange registered with the Securities and Exchange Commission as a national securities exchange for purposes of the Securities Exchange Act of 1934 and any German stock exchange on which registered dealings in shares takes place. The term also includes any other stock exchange agreed upon by the competent authorities of the Contracting States.

If a company has only one class of shares, it is only necessary to consider whether the shares of that class meet the relevant trading requirements. If the company has more than one class of shares, it is necessary as an initial matter to determine which class or classes constitute the "principal class of shares." The term "principal class of shares" is defined in clause (b)(aa) of paragraph 8 to mean the ordinary or common shares of the company representing the majority of the aggregate voting power and value of the company. If the company does not have a class of ordinary or common shares representing the majority of the aggregate voting power and value of the company, then the "principal class of shares" is that class or any combination of classes of shares that represents, in the aggregate, a majority of the voting power and value of the company. Although in a particular case involving a company with several classes of shares it is conceivable that more than one group of classes could be identified that account for more than 50% of the shares, it is only necessary for one such group to satisfy the requirements of this subparagraph in order for the company to be entitled to benefits. Benefits would not be denied to the company even if a second, non-qualifying, group of shares with more than half of the company's voting power and value could be identified. Clause (c)(bb) of paragraph 8 defines the term "shares" to include depository receipts for shares or trust certificates for shares.

A company whose principal class of shares is regularly traded on a recognized stock exchange will nevertheless not qualify for benefits under subparagraph (c) of paragraph 2 if it has a disproportionate class of shares that is not regularly traded on a recognized stock exchange. The term "disproportionate class of shares" is defined in subparagraph (c) of paragraph 8. A company has a disproportionate class of shares if it has outstanding a class of shares that is subject to terms or other arrangements that entitle the holder to a larger portion of the company's income, profit, or gain in the other Contracting State than that to which the holder would be entitled in the absence of such terms or arrangements. Thus, for example, a company resident in the Federal Republic of Germany meets the test of subparagraph (c) of paragraph 8 if it has outstanding a class of "tracking stock" that pays dividends based upon a formula that approximates the company's return on its assets employed in the United States.

The following example illustrates this result.

Example. GCo is a corporation resident in the Federal Republic of Germany. GCo has two classes of shares: Common and Preferred. The Common shares are listed and regularly traded on the Frankfurt Stockholm Stock Exchange. The Preferred shares have no voting rights and are entitled to receive dividends equal in amount to interest payments that GCo receives from unrelated borrowers in the United States. The Preferred shares are owned entirely by a single investor that is a resident of a country with which the United States does not have a tax treaty. The Common shares account for more than 50 percent of the value of GCo and for 100 percent of the voting power. Because the owner of the Preferred shares is entitled to receive payments corresponding to the U.S. source interest income earned by GCo, the Preferred shares are a disproportionate class of shares. Because the Preferred shares are not regularly traded on a recognized stock exchange, GCo will not qualify for benefits under subparagraph (c) of paragraph 2.

The term "regularly traded" is not defined in the Convention. In accordance with paragraph 2 of Article 3 (General Definitions), this term will be defined by reference to the domestic tax laws of the State from which treaty benefits are sought, generally the source State. In the case of the United States, this term is understood to have the meaning it has under Treas. Reg. section 1.884-5(d)(4)(i)(B), relating to the branch tax provisions of the Code. Under these regulations, a class of shares is considered to be "regularly traded" if two requirements are met: trades in the class of shares are made in more than *de minimis* quantities on at least 60 days during the taxable year, and the aggregate number of shares in the class traded during the year is at least 10 percent of the average number of shares outstanding during the year. Sections 1.884-5(d)(4)(i)(A), (ii) and (iii) will not be taken into account for purposes of defining the term "regularly traded" under the Convention.

The regular trading requirement can be met by trading on any recognized exchange or exchanges. Trading on one or more recognized stock exchanges may be aggregated for purposes of this requirement. Thus, a U.S. company could satisfy the regularly traded requirement through trading, in whole or in part, on a recognized stock exchange located in the Federal Republic of Germany. Authorized but unissued shares are not considered for purposes of this test.

The term "primarily traded" is not defined in the Convention. In accordance with paragraph 2 of Article 3 (General Definitions), this term will have the meaning it has under the laws of the State concerning the taxes to which the Convention applies, generally the source State. In the case of the United States, this term is understood to have the meaning it has under Treas. Reg. section 1.884-5(d)(3), relating to the branch tax provisions of the Code. Accordingly, stock of a corporation is "primarily traded" on a recognized stock exchange located in the State of residence if the number of shares in the company's principal class of shares that are traded during the taxable year on all recognized stock exchanges in the State of residence exceeds the number of shares in the company's principal class of shares that are traded during that year on established securities markets in any other single foreign country.

A company whose principal class of shares is regularly traded on a recognized exchange but cannot meet the primarily traded test may claim treaty benefits if its primary place of management and control is in its country of residence. This test should be distinguished from the "place of effective management" test which is used in the OECD Model and by many other countries to establish residence. In some cases, the place of effective management test has been interpreted to mean the place where the board of directors meets. By contrast, the primary place of management and control test looks to where day-to-day responsibility for the management of the company (and its subsidiaries) is exercised. The company's primary place of management and control will be located in the State in which the company is a resident only if the executive officers and senior management employees exercise day-to-day responsibility for more of the strategic, financial and operational policy decision making for the company (including direct and indirect subsidiaries) in that State than in the other State or any third state, and the staff that support the management in making those decisions are also based in that State. Thus, the test looks to the overall activities of the relevant persons to see where those activities are conducted. In most cases, it will be a necessary, but not a sufficient, condition that the headquarters of the company (that is, the place at which the CEO and other top executives normally are based) be located in the Contracting State of which the company is a resident.

To apply the test, it will be necessary to determine which persons are to be considered "executive officers and senior management employees". In most cases, it will not be necessary to look beyond the executives who are members of the Board of Directors (the "inside directors") in the case of a U.S. company. That will not always be the case, however; in fact, the relevant persons may be employees of subsidiaries if those persons make the strategic, financial and operational policy decisions. Moreover, it would be necessary to take into account any special voting arrangements that result in certain board members making certain decisions without the participation of other board members.

Subsidiaries of Publicly-Traded Corporations -- Subparagraph 2(c)(bb)

A company resident in a Contracting State is entitled to all the benefits of the Convention under clause (bb) of subparagraph (c) of paragraph 2 if five or fewer publicly traded companies described in clause (i) are the direct or indirect owners of at least 50 percent of the aggregate vote and value of the company's shares (and at least 50 percent of any disproportionate class of shares). If the publicly-traded companies are indirect owners, however, each of the intermediate companies must be a resident of one of the Contracting States.

Thus, for example, a German company, all the shares of which are owned by another German company, would qualify for benefits under the Convention if the principal class of shares (and any disproportionate classes of shares) of the German parent company are regularly and primarily traded on the London stock exchange. However, a German subsidiary would not qualify for benefits under clause (ii) if the publicly traded parent company were a resident of Ireland, for example, and not a resident of the United States or Germany. Furthermore, if a German parent company indirectly owned a German company through a chain of subsidiaries, each such subsidiary in the chain, as an intermediate owner, must be a resident of the United States or Germany for the German subsidiary to meet the test in clause (bb).

Tax-Exempt Organizations -- Subparagraph 2(d)

The Contracting States agreed that certain tax-exempt organizations should be entitled to all the benefits of the Convention, without regard to the residence of beneficiaries or members. Entities qualifying under this subparagraph are those that are organized under the laws of one of the Contracting States and established and maintained in that Contracting State exclusively for a religious, charitable, educational, scientific, or other similar purpose.

Pension Funds -- Subparagraph 2(e)

An entity organized under the laws of one of the Contracting States and established and maintained in that Contracting State to provide, pursuant to a plan, pension or other similar benefits to employed and self-employed persons, provided that more than 50 percent of the beneficiaries, members or participants of the entity are individuals resident in either Contracting State or if the organization sponsoring such person is entitled to all the benefits of the Convention under paragraph 2 of Article 28. For purposes of this provision, the term "beneficiaries" should be understood to refer to the persons receiving benefits from the entity.

Ownership/Base Erosion -- Subparagraph 2(f)

Subparagraph 2(f) provides an additional method to qualify for treaty benefits that applies to any form of legal entity that is a resident of a Contracting State. The test provided in subparagraph (f), the so-called ownership and base erosion test, is a two-part test. Both prongs of the test must be satisfied for the resident to be entitled to treaty benefits under subparagraph 2(f).

The ownership prong of the test, under clause (aa), requires that 50 percent or more of each class of shares or other beneficial interests in the person is owned, directly or indirectly, on at least half the days of the person's taxable year by persons who are residents of the Contracting State of which that person is a resident and that are themselves entitled to treaty benefits under certain parts of paragraph 2 -- subparagraphs (a), (b), (d), (e), or clause (aa) of subparagraph (c). In the case of indirect owners, however, each of the intermediate owners must be a resident of that Contracting State.

Trusts may be entitled to benefits under this provision if they are treated as residents under Article 4 (Residence) and they otherwise satisfy the requirements of this subparagraph. For purposes of this subparagraph, the beneficial interests in a trust will be considered to be owned by its beneficiaries in proportion to each beneficiary's actuarial interest in the trust. The interest of a remainder beneficiary will be equal to 100 percent less the aggregate percentages held by income beneficiaries. A beneficiary's interest in a trust will not be considered to be owned by a person entitled to benefits under the other provisions of paragraph 2 if it is not possible to determine the beneficiary's actuarial interest. Consequently, if it is not possible to determine the actuarial interest of the beneficiaries in a trust, the ownership test under clause (aa) cannot be satisfied, unless all possible beneficiaries are persons entitled to benefits under the specified subparagraphs of paragraph 2.

The base erosion prong of clause (bb) of subparagraph (f) is satisfied with respect to a person if less than 50 percent of the person's gross income for the taxable year, as determined under the tax law in the person's State of residence, is paid or accrued, directly or indirectly, to persons who are not residents of either Contracting State entitled to treaty benefits under subparagraph (a), (b), (d), (e), or clause (aa) of subparagraph (c), in the form of payments deductible for tax purposes in the person's State of residence. To the extent they are deductible from the taxable base, trust distributions are deductible payments. However, depreciation and amortization deductions, which do not represent payments or accruals to other persons, are disregarded for this purpose.

Paragraph 3

Paragraph 3 sets forth a derivative benefits test that is potentially applicable to all treaty benefits, although the test is applied to individual items of income. In general, a derivative benefits test entitles the resident of a Contracting State to treaty benefits if the owner of the resident would have been entitled to the same benefit had the income in question flowed directly to that owner. To qualify under this paragraph, the company must meet an ownership test and a base erosion test.

Subparagraph (a) sets forth the ownership test. Under this test, seven or fewer equivalent beneficiaries must own shares representing at least 95 percent of the aggregate voting power and value of the company and at least 50 percent of any disproportionate class of shares. Ownership may be direct or indirect. The term "equivalent beneficiary" is defined in subparagraph (e) of paragraph 8. This definition may be met in two alternative ways, the first of which has two requirements.

Under the first alternative, a person may be an equivalent beneficiary because it is entitled to equivalent benefits under a treaty between the country of source and the country in which the person is a resident. This alternative has two requirements.

The first requirement is that the person must be a resident of a member state of the European Union, a European Economic Area state, or a party to the North American Free Trade Agreement (collectively, "qualifying States").

The second requirement of the first alternative is that the person must be entitled to equivalent benefits under an applicable treaty. To satisfy the second requirement, the person must be entitled to all the benefits of a comprehensive treaty between the Contracting State from which benefits of the Convention are claimed and a qualifying State under provisions that are analogous to the rules in paragraph 2 of this Article regarding individuals, governments, publicly-traded companies, tax-exempt organizations, and pension funds. If the treaty in question does not have a comprehensive limitation on benefits article, this requirement is met only if the person would be entitled to treaty benefits under the tests in paragraph 2 of this Article applicable to individuals, governments, publicly-traded companies, tax-exempt organizations and pension funds. if the person were a resident of one of the Contracting States.

In order to satisfy the second requirement of the first alternative with respect to insurance premiums, dividends, interest, royalties, or branch tax, paragraph 8(e)(aa)(B) provides that the person must be entitled to a rate of tax that is at least as low as the tax rate that would apply under the Convention to such income. Thus, the rates to be compared are: (1) the rate of tax that the source State would have imposed if a qualified resident of the other Contracting State was the beneficial owner of the income; and (2) the rate of tax that the source State would have imposed if the third State resident received the income directly from the source State. For example, USCo is a wholly owned subsidiary of GCo, a company resident in the Federal Republic of Germany. GCo is wholly owned by ICo, a corporation resident in Italy. Assuming GCo satisfies the requirements of paragraph 3 of Article 10 (Dividends), GCo would be eligible for the elimination of dividend withholding tax. The dividend withholding tax rate in the treaty between the United States and Italy is 5 percent. Thus, if ICo received the dividend directly from USCo, ICo would have been subject to a 5 percent rate of withholding tax on the dividend. Because ICo would not be entitled to a rate of withholding tax that is at least as low as the rate that would apply under the Convention to such income (i.e., zero), ICo is not an equivalent beneficiary within the meaning of paragraph 8(g)(aa) of Article 28 with respect to the elimination of withholding tax on dividends.

Subparagraph 8(f) provides a special rule to take account of the fact that withholding taxes on many inter-company dividends, interest and royalties are exempt within the European Union by reason of various EU directives, rather than by tax treaty. If a U.S. company receives such payments from a German company, and that U.S. company is owned by a company resident in a member state of the European Union that would have qualified for an exemption from withholding tax if it had received the income directly, the parent company will be treated as an equivalent beneficiary. This rule is necessary because many European Union member countries have not re-negotiated their tax treaties to reflect the rates applicable under the directives.

The requirement that a person be entitled to "all the benefits" of a comprehensive tax treaty eliminates those persons that qualify for benefits with respect to only certain types of income. Accordingly, the fact that a French parent of a German company is engaged in the active conduct of a trade or business in France and therefore would be entitled to the benefits of the U.S.-France treaty if it received dividends directly from a U.S. subsidiary of the German company is not sufficient for purposes of this paragraph. Further, the French company cannot be an equivalent beneficiary if it qualifies for benefits only with respect to certain income as a result of a "derivative benefits" provision in the U.S.-France treaty. However, it would be possible to look through the French company to its parent company to determine whether the parent company is an equivalent beneficiary.

The second alternative for satisfying the "equivalent beneficiary" test is available only to residents of one of the two Contracting States. U.S. or German residents who are eligible for treaty benefits by reason of subparagraphs (a), (b), (c)(aa), (d), or (e) of paragraph 2 are equivalent beneficiaries under the second alternative. Thus, a German individual will be an equivalent beneficiary without regard to whether the individual would have been entitled to receive the same benefits if it received the income directly. A resident of a third country cannot qualify for treaty benefits under any of those subparagraphs or any other rule of the treaty, and therefore would not qualify as an equivalent beneficiary under this alternative. Thus, a resident of a third country can be an equivalent beneficiary only if it would have been entitled to equivalent benefits had it received the income directly.

The second alternative was included in order to clarify that ownership by certain residents of a Contracting State would not disqualify a U.S. or German company under this paragraph. Thus, for example, if 90 percent of a German company is owned by five companies that are resident in member states of the European Union who satisfy the requirements of clause (aa), and 10 percent of the German company is owned by a U.S. or German individual, then the German company still can satisfy the requirements of subparagraph (a) of paragraph 3.

Subparagraph (b) of paragraph 3 sets forth the base erosion test. A company meets this base erosion test if less than 50 percent of its gross income, as determined under the tax law in the company's State of residence, for the taxable period is paid or accrued, directly or indirectly, to a person or persons who are not equivalent beneficiaries in the form of payments deductible for tax purposes in company's State of residence. This test is the same as the base erosion test in clause (bb) of subparagraph (f) of paragraph 2, except that the test in subparagraph 3(b) focuses on base-eroding payments to persons who are not equivalent beneficiaries.

Paragraph 4

Paragraph 4 sets forth an alternative test under which a resident of a Contracting State may receive treaty benefits with respect to certain items of income that are connected to an active trade or business conducted in its State of residence. A resident of a Contracting State may qualify for benefits under paragraph 4 whether or not it also qualifies under paragraphs 2 or 3.

Subparagraph (a) sets forth the general rule that a resident of a Contracting State engaged in the active conduct of a trade or business in that State may obtain the benefits of the Convention with respect to an item of income, profit, or gain derived from the other Contracting State. The item of income, profit, or gain, however, must be derived in connection with or incidental to that trade or business.

The term "trade or business" is not defined in the Convention. Pursuant to paragraph 2 of Article 3 (General Definitions), when determining whether a resident of the Federal Republic of Germany is entitled to the benefits of the Convention under paragraph 4 of this Article with respect to an item of income derived from sources within the United States, the United States will ascribe to this term the meaning that it has under the law of the United States. Accordingly, the U.S. competent authority will refer to the regulations issued under section 367(a) for the definition of the term "trade or business." In general, therefore, a trade or business will be considered to be a specific unified group of activities that constitute or could constitute an independent economic enterprise carried on for profit. Furthermore, a corporation generally will be considered to carry on a trade or business only if the officers and employees of the corporation conduct substantial managerial and operational activities.

The business of making or managing investments for the resident's own account will be considered to be a trade or business only when part of banking, insurance or securities activities conducted by a bank, an insurance company, or a registered securities dealer. Such activities conducted by a person other than a bank, insurance company or registered securities dealer will not be considered to be the conduct of an active trade or business, nor would they be considered to be the conduct of an active trade or business if conducted by a bank, insurance company or registered securities dealer but not as part of the company's banking, insurance or dealer business. . Because a headquarters operation is in the business of managing investments, a company that functions solely as a headquarters company will not be considered to be engaged in an active trade or business for purposes of paragraph 4.

An item of income is derived in connection with a trade or business if the income-producing activity in the State of source is a line of business that "forms a part of" or is "complementary" to the trade or business conducted in the State of residence by the income recipient.

A business activity generally will be considered to form part of a business activity conducted in the State of source if the two activities involve the design, manufacture or sale of the same products or type of products, or the provision of similar services. The line of business in the State of residence may be upstream, downstream, or parallel to the activity conducted in the State of source. Thus, the line of business may provide inputs for a manufacturing process that occurs in the State of source, may sell the output of that manufacturing process, or simply may sell the same sorts of products that are being sold by the trade or business carried on in the State of source.

Example 1. USCo is a corporation resident in the United States. USCo is engaged in an active manufacturing business in the United States. USCo owns 100 percent of the shares of GCo, a company resident in the Federal Republic of Germany. GCo distributes USCo products in Germany. Because the business activities conducted by the two corporations involve the same products, GCo's distribution business is considered to form a part of USCo's manufacturing business.

Example 2. The facts are the same as in Example 1, except that USCo does not manufacture. Rather, USCo operates a large research and development facility in the United States that licenses intellectual property to affiliates worldwide, including GCo. GCo and other USCo affiliates then manufacture and market the USCo-designed products in their respective markets. Because the activities conducted by GCo and USCo involve the same product lines, these activities are considered to form a part of the same trade or business.

For two activities to be considered to be "complementary," the activities need not relate to the same types of products or services, but they should be part of the same overall industry and be related in the sense that the success or failure of one activity will tend to result in success or failure for the other. Where more than one trade or business is conducted in the State of source and only one of the trades or businesses forms a part of or is complementary to a trade or business conducted in the State of residence, it is necessary to identify the trade or business to which an item of income is attributable. Royalties generally will be considered to be derived in connection with the trade or business to which the underlying intangible property is attributable. Dividends will be deemed to be derived first out of earnings and profits of the treaty-benefited trade or business, and then out of other earnings and profits. Interest income may be allocated under any reasonable method consistently applied. A method that conforms to U.S. principles for expense allocation will be considered a reasonable method.

Example 3. Americair is a corporation resident in the United States that operates an international airline. GSub is a wholly-owned subsidiary of Americair resident in the Federal Republic of Germany. SSub operates a chain of hotels in the Federal Republic of Germany that are located near airports served by Americair flights. Americair frequently sells tour packages that include air travel to the Federal Republic of Germany and lodging at GSub hotels. Although both companies are engaged in the active conduct of a trade or business, the businesses of operating a chain of hotels and operating an airline are distinct trades or businesses. Therefore GSub's business does not form a part of Americair's business. However, GSub's business is considered to be complementary to Americair's business because they are part of the same overall industry (travel), and the links between their operations tend to make them interdependent.

Example 4. The facts are the same as in Example 3, except that GSub owns an office building in the Federal Republic of Germany instead of a hotel chain. No part of Americair's business is conducted through the office building. GSub's business is not considered to form a part of or to be complementary to Americair's business. They are engaged in distinct trades or businesses in separate industries, and there is no economic dependence between the two operations.

Example 5. USFlower is a company resident in the United States. USFlower produces and sells flowers in the United States and other countries. USFlower owns all the shares of GHolding, a corporation resident in the Federal Republic of Germany. GHolding is a holding company that is not engaged in a trade or business. GHolding owns all the shares of three corporations that are resident in the Federal Republic of Germany: GFlower, GLawn, and GFish. GFlower distributes USFlower flowers under the USFlower trademark in the Federal Republic of Germany. GLawn markets a line of lawn care products in the Federal Republic of Germany under the USFlower trademark. In addition to being sold under the same trademark, GLawn and GFlower products are sold in the same stores and sales of each company's products tend to generate increased sales of the other's products. GFish imports fish from the United States and distributes it to fish wholesalers in the Federal Republic of Germany. For purposes of paragraph 4, the business of GFlower forms a part of the business of USFlower, the business of GLawn is complementary to the business of USFlower, and the business of GFish is neither part of nor complementary to that of USFlower.

An item of income derived from the State of source is "incidental to" the trade or business carried on in the State of residence if production of the item facilitates the conduct of the trade or business in the State of residence. An example of incidental income is the temporary investment of working capital of a person in the State of residence in securities issued by persons in the State of source.

Subparagraph (b) of paragraph 4 states a further condition to the general rule in subparagraph (a) in cases where the trade or business generating the item of income in question is carried on either by the person deriving the income or by any associated enterprises. Subparagraph (b) states that the trade or business carried on in the State of residence, under these circumstances, must be substantial in relation to the activity in the State of source. The substantiality requirement is intended to prevent a narrow case of treaty-shopping abuses in which a company attempts to qualify for benefits by engaging in de minimis connected business activities in the treaty country in which it is resident (i.e., activities that have little economic cost or effect with respect to the company business as a whole).

The determination of substantiality is made based upon all the facts and circumstances and takes into account the comparative sizes of the trades or businesses in each Contracting State , the nature of the activities performed in each Contracting State, and the relative contributions made to that trade or business in each Contracting State. In any case, in making each determination or comparison, due regard will be given to the relative sizes of the U.S. and German economies.

The determination in subparagraph (b) also is made separately for each item of income derived from the State of source. It therefore is possible that a person would be entitled to the benefits of the Convention with respect to one item of income but not with respect to another. If a resident of a Contracting State is entitled to treaty benefits with respect to a particular item of income under paragraph 4, the resident is entitled to all benefits of the Convention insofar as they affect the taxation of that item of income in the State of source.

The application of the substantiality requirement only to income from related parties focuses only on potential abuse cases, and does not hamper certain other kinds of non-abusive activities, even though the income recipient resident in a Contracting State may be very small in relation to the entity generating income in the other Contracting State. For example, if a small U.S. research firm develops a process that it licenses to a very large, unrelated, German pharmaceutical manufacturer, the size of the U.S. research firm would not have to be tested against the size of the German manufacturer. Similarly, a small U.S. bank that makes a loan to a very large unrelated German business would not have to pass a substantiality test to receive treaty benefits under paragraph 4.

Subparagraph (c) of paragraph 4 provides special attribution rules for purposes of applying the substantive rules of subparagraphs (a) and (b). Thus, these rules apply for purposes of determining whether a person meets the requirement in subparagraph (a) that it be engaged in the active conduct of a trade or business and that the item of income is derived in connection with that active trade or business, and for making the comparison required by the "substantiality" requirement in subparagraph (b). Subparagraph (c) attributes the activities of a partnership to each of its partners. Subparagraph (c) also attributes to a person activities conducted by persons "connected" to such person. A person ("X") is connected to another person ("Y") if X possesses 50 percent or more of the beneficial interest in Y (or if Y possesses 50 percent or more of the beneficial interest in X). For this purpose, X is connected to a company if X owns shares representing fifty percent or more of the aggregate voting power and value of the company or fifty percent or more of the beneficial equity interest in the company. X also is connected to Y if a third person possesses fifty percent or more of the beneficial interest in both X and Y. For this purpose, if X or Y is a company, the threshold relationship with respect to such company or companies is fifty percent or more of the aggregate voting power and value or fifty percent or more of the beneficial equity interest. Finally, X is connected to Y if, based upon all the facts and circumstances, X controls Y, Y controls X, or X and Y are controlled by the same person or persons.

Paragraph 5

Paragraph 5 deals with the treatment of income in the context of a so-called "triangular case."

The term "triangular case" refers to the use of the following structure by a resident of the Federal Republic of Germany to earn, in the example, interest income from the United States. The German resident, who is assumed to qualify for benefits under one or more of the provisions of Article 28 (Limitation on Benefits), sets up a permanent establishment in a third jurisdiction that imposes only a low rate of tax on the income of the permanent establishment. The German resident lends funds into the United States through the permanent establishment. The permanent establishment, despite its third-jurisdiction location, is an integral part of a German resident. Therefore the income that it earns on those loans, absent the provisions of paragraph 5, is entitled to exemption from U.S. withholding tax under the Convention. Under a German tax treaty with the host jurisdiction of the permanent establishment, the income of the permanent establishment is exempt from German tax. Thus, the interest income is exempt from U.S. tax, is subject to little tax in the host jurisdiction of the permanent establishment, and is exempt from German tax.

Paragraph 5 replaces the otherwise applicable rules in the Convention for dividends, interest and royalties with a 15 percent withholding tax for these amounts and the domestic law rules of the source country for any other income, if the actual tax paid on the income in the country of residence of the enterprise and in the third jurisdiction is less than 60 percent of the tax that would have been payable in the country of residence of the enterprise if the income were earned in such country by the enterprise and were not attributable to the permanent establishment in the third state.

In general, the principles employed under Code section 954(b)(4) will be employed to determine whether the profits are subject to an effective rate of taxation that is above the specified threshold.

Notwithstanding the level of tax on income of the permanent establishment, paragraph 5 does not apply under certain circumstances. In the case of royalties, paragraph 5 does not apply if the royalties are received as compensation for the use of, or the right to use, intangible property produced or developed by the permanent establishment itself. In the case of other income, paragraph 5 does not apply if the income is derived in connection with, or is incidental to, the active conduct of a trade or business carried on by the permanent establishment in the third state. The business of making, managing or simply holding investments for the person's own account is not considered to be an active trade or business, unless these are banking or securities activities carried on by a bank or registered securities dealer.

Paragraph 6

Paragraph 6 provides that German Investment Funds or German *Investmentaktiengesellschaft* (collectively referred to as *Investmentvermögen*) may only be granted the benefits of the Convention if at least 90 percent of the shares or other beneficial interests in the German *Investmentvermögen* are owned directly or indirectly by German residents that are entitled to the benefits of this Convention under certain subparagraphs of paragraph 2 of this Article (i.e., subparagraphs (a), (b), (d) or (e) and clause aa) of paragraph (c)) or by persons that are equivalent beneficiaries with respect to the income derived by the German *Investmentvermögen* for which benefits are being claimed. For purposes of this paragraph, beneficiaries of entities that are subject to numbers 3 and 5 of paragraph 1 of section 1 of the German Corporate Tax Act shall be treated as indirectly owning shares of a German *Investmentvermögen*. Foundations referred to in number 5 of paragraph 1 of section 1 of the German Corporate Tax Act, other than those referred to in subparagraph d) of paragraph 2 of this Article shall not be take into account in determining whether a German *Investmentvermögen* meets the 90 percent threshold. Paragraph 24 of Article XVI of the Protocol provides that the competent authorities will establish procedures for determining indirect ownership for purposes of determining whether the 90 percent ownership threshold of paragraph 6 is met and that it is anticipated that such procedures may include statistically valid sampling techniques.

Paragraph 7

Paragraph 7 provides that a resident of one of the Contracting States that is not entitled to the benefits of the Convention as a result of paragraphs 1 through 6 still may be granted benefits under the Convention at the discretion of the competent authority of the State from which benefits are claimed. In making determinations under paragraph 7, that competent authority will take into account as its guideline whether the establishment, acquisition, or maintenance of the person seeking benefits under the Convention, or the conduct of such person's operations, has or had as one of its principal purposes the obtaining of benefits under the Convention. Benefits will not be granted, however, solely because a company was established prior to the effective date of a treaty or protocol. In that case a company would still be required to establish to the satisfaction of the Competent Authority clear non-tax business reasons for its formation in a Contracting State, or that the allowance of benefits would not otherwise be contrary to the purposes of the treaty. Thus, persons that establish operations in one of the States with a principal purpose of obtaining the benefits of the Convention ordinarily will not be granted relief under paragraph 7.

The competent authority's discretion is quite broad. It may grant all of the benefits of the Convention to the taxpayer making the request, or it may grant only certain benefits. For instance, it may grant benefits only with respect to a particular item of income in a manner similar to paragraph 4. Further, the competent authority may establish conditions, such as setting time limits on the duration of any relief granted.

For purposes of implementing paragraph 7, a taxpayer will be permitted to present his case to the relevant competent authority for an advance determination based on the facts. In these circumstances, it is also expected that, if the competent authority determines that benefits are to be allowed, they will be allowed retroactively to the time of entry into force of the relevant treaty provision or the establishment of the structure in question, whichever is later. Before denying benefits of the Convention under this paragraph, the competent authority will consult with the competent authority of the other Contracting State.

Finally, there may be cases in which a resident of a Contracting State may apply for discretionary relief to the competent authority of his State of residence. This would arise, for example, if the benefit it is claiming is provided by the residence country, and not by the source country. So, for example, if a company that is a resident of the United States would like to claim the benefit of the re-sourcing rule of paragraph 2 of Article 23, but it does not meet any of the objective tests of this Article, it may apply to the U.S. competent authority for discretionary relief.

Paragraph 8

Paragraph 8 defines several key terms for purposes of Article 28. Each of the defined terms is discussed in the context in which it is used.

Article XV

Article XV of the Protocol updates several references in the Convention that have become outdated since the Euro has replaced the German mark as the currency of the Federal Republic of Germany.

Article XVI

Article XVI of the Protocol restates and updates the Protocol to the Convention. The following description of Article XVI only discusses the aspect of Article XVI that amends the Protocol to the Convention and that has not been described elsewhere in the technical explanation. Consequently, only paragraphs 21 and 23 of the Article are described below.

Paragraph 21

Paragraph 21 makes clear that paragraph 4 of Article 24 does not obligate a Contracting State to permit cross-border consolidation of income or similar benefits between enterprises.

Paragraph 23

Paragraph 23 makes clear that Article 26 (Exchange of Information and Administrative Assistance) provides the competent authority of each Contracting State the power to obtain and provide information held by financial institutions, nominees, or persons acting in an agency or fiduciary capacity (not including information that would reveal confidential communications between a client and an attorney, solicitor, or other legal representative, where the client seeks legal advice), or respecting interests in a person, including bearer shares, regardless of any laws or practices of the requested State that might otherwise preclude the obtaining of such information. Thus, such information must be provided to the requesting State notwithstanding the fact that disclosure of the information is precluded by bank secrecy or similar legislation relating to disclosure of financial information by financial institutions or intermediaries.

Article XVII

Article XVII of the Protocol contains the rules for bringing the Protocol into force and giving effect to its provisions.

Paragraph 1

Paragraph 1 provides for the ratification of the Convention by both Contracting States according to their constitutional and statutory requirements. Instruments of ratification shall be exchanged as soon as possible.

In the United States, the process leading to ratification and entry into force is as follows: Once a treaty has been signed by authorized representatives of the two Contracting States, the Department of State sends the treaty to the President who formally transmits it to the Senate for its advice and consent to ratification, which requires approval by two-thirds of the Senators present and voting. Prior to this vote, however, it generally has been the practice for the Senate Committee on Foreign Relations to hold hearings on the treaty and make a recommendation regarding its approval to the full Senate. Both Government and private sector witnesses may testify at these hearings. After the Senate gives its advice and consent to ratification of the protocol or treaty, an instrument of ratification is drafted for the President's signature. The President's signature completes the process in the United States.

Paragraph 2

Paragraph 2 provides that the Protocol will enter into force upon the exchange of instruments of ratification. The date on which a Protocol enters into force is not necessarily the date on which its provisions take effect. Paragraph 2, therefore, also contains rules that determine when the provisions of the Protocol will have effect.

Under subparagraph 2(a), the Protocol will have effect with respect to taxes withheld at source (principally dividends and interest) for amounts paid or credited on or after the first day of January of the year in which the Protocol enters into force. For example, if instruments of ratification are exchanged on April 25 of a given year, the withholding rates specified in paragraph 2 and 3 of Article 10 (Dividends) would be applicable to any dividends paid or credited on or after January 1 of that year. This rule allows the benefits of the withholding reductions to be put into effect for the entire year the Protocol enters into force. If a withholding agent withholds at a higher rate than that provided by the Protocol (e.g., for payments made before April 25 in the example above), a beneficial owner of the income that is a resident of the Federal Republic of Germany may make a claim for refund pursuant to section 1464 of the Code.

Under subparagraph 2(b), the Protocol will have effect with respect to taxes other than those withheld at source for any taxable period beginning on or after January 1 of the year next following entry into force of the Protocol. With respect to taxes on capital, the Convention will have effect for taxes levied on items of capital owned on or after January 1 next following the entry into force of the Protocol.

Paragraph 3

Paragraph 3 provides two exceptions to the effective date rules of paragraph 2. The provisions of paragraphs 2 and 3 of Article 1 (General Scope) will have effect after the entry into force of the Protocol and apply in respect of any tax claim irrespective of whether the tax claim pre-dates the entry into force of the Protocol (or the effective date of any of its provisions). In addition, paragraph 3 provides that the amendments made to Article 19 (Government Service) by Article X of the Protocol do not have effect with respect to individuals who at the time of the signing of the Convention on August 29, 1989 were employed by the United States, a political subdivision or local authority thereof.

Paragraph 4

Paragraph 4 provides a specific effective date for purposes of the binding arbitration provisions of Article 25 (Mutual Agreement Procedure) (Article XIII of the Protocol). Paragraph 4 provides that Article XIII of the Protocol is effective for cases (i) that are under consideration by the competent authorities as of the date on which the Protocol enters into force and (ii) cases that come under such consideration after the Protocol enters into force. In addition, paragraph 4 provides that the commencement date for cases that are under consideration by the competent authorities as of the date on which the Protocol enters into force is the date the Protocol enters into force. As a result, cases that are unresolved as of the entry into force of the Protocol will go into binding arbitration no later than two years after the entry into force of the Protocol, if the cases are not otherwise resolved through the competent authority procedure. Pursuant to clause c)aa) of paragraph 6 of Article 25, the competent authorities may agree to any earlier date.

Paragraph 5

As in many recent U.S. treaties, however, paragraph 5 also provides an additional exception to paragraph 2. Under paragraph 5, if the Convention as unmodified by the Protocol would have afforded any person that was entitled to benefits under the unmodified Convention greater relief from tax than under the Convention as modified by the Protocol, the unmodified Convention shall, at the election of such person, continue to have effect in its entirety for a 12-month period from the date on which the provisions of the Protocol would have otherwise had effect with respect to such person.

Thus, a taxpayer who was entitled to benefits may elect to extend the benefits of the unmodified Convention for one year from the date on which the relevant provision of the modified Convention would first take effect. During the period in which the election is in effect, the provisions of the unmodified Convention will continue to apply only insofar as they applied before the entry into force of the Protocol. If the grace period is elected, all of the provisions of the unmodified Convention must be applied for that additional year. The taxpayer may not apply certain, more favorable provisions of the unmodified Convention and, at the same time, apply other, more favorable provisions of the modified Convention. The taxpayer must choose one regime or the other.

For example, suppose the instruments of ratification are exchanged on April 1, 2007 and the Protocol thus enters into force on that date. The Protocol would take effect with respect to taxes withheld at source for amounts paid or credited on or after January 1, 2007. With respect to other income taxes, the Protocol would be applicable for taxable years beginning on or after January 1, 2008. If the election is made, the provisions of the unmodified Convention would continue to have effect (i) regarding withholding, for amounts paid or credited at any time prior to January 1, 2008, and (ii) regarding other income taxes, for fiscal periods beginning before January 1, 2009; the provisions of the Protocol (including the rules of Article 28 (Limitation on Benefits)) would have effect (i) regarding withholding, for amounts paid or credited on or after

January 1, 2008, and (ii) regarding other income taxes, for fiscal periods beginning on or after January 1, 2009.

Paragraph 6

Paragraph 6 provides that the following notes exchanged with respect to the current Convention will cease to have effect when the provisions of the Protocol take effect in accord with this Article: (i) the notes exchanged on August 29, 1989 and (ii) the German note of November 3, 1989.

www.ingramcontent.com/pod-product-compliance
Lightning Source LLC
Chambersburg PA
CBHW080543290526
45790CB00006B/2532